★

FROM CYD CHARISSE
TO *PSYCHO*

★

★

FROM CYD CHARISSE
TO *PSYCHO*

Dale Thomajan

★

Walker and Company
New York

First published in the United States of America in 1992
by Walker Publishing Company, Inc.

Published simultaneously in Canada by Thomas Allen & Son
Canada, Limited, Markham, Ontario

Library of Congress Cataloging-in-Publication Data
Thomajan, Dale.
From Cyd Charisse to *Psycho* / Dale Thomajan.
p. cm.
ISBN 0-8027-1213-4 —ISBN 0-8027-7382-6 (pbk)
1. Motion pictures—Miscellanea. I. Title.
PN1998.T436 1992
791.43—dc20 92-15758
CIP

Book Design by Poul Lange, Ivy Design

Printed in the United States of America

2   4   6   8   10   9   7   5   3   1

A longer version of "The Best Suspense Thriller" appeared under the title
"Clouzot's Wild Bunch" in the November–December 1991 issue of *Film Comment*.

A shorter version of "The Best Advice You'll Ever Receive on How to Behave in
Old-Movie Theaters" appeared under the title "Old-Movie Etiquette" in the
February 1988 issue of *Spy*.

Many of the photos in this book are from the collection of
the Film Society of Lincoln Center.

This book is dedicated to
Bergie Thomajan, the world's best mother
on or off screen,
and to
the memory of my father, Zareh Thomajan, who without
realizing it taught me practically everything I know about
writing.

★
CONTENTS
★

CONTENTS

II. PEOPLE

III. ODDS AND ENDS

★

ACKNOWLEDGMENTS

★

For their generous contributions, the author would like to thank Arto DeMirjian, Jr.; Ed Chilcott; Linda Donald; William K. Everson; Timothy Hamilton; Mary K. Herbert and Kevin Sullivan of Walker and Company; Wendy Keys and Jim Bouras of the Film Society of Lincoln Center; Richard Sasnow; Donald Silva; Whitey St. Claire; and, especially, Richard T. Jameson, not only for his foreword but for his support in general.

★

FOREWORD

★

Dale Thomajan. I remember the first time I encountered the name. It was the mid-1970s, I was editing a "little magazine" in Seattle called *Movietone News*, and an envelope arrived in the mail. Inside were a letter proposing a column of aphoristic observations on movies plus several issues' worth of installments, should I choose to run them. I chose not to; I had taken my pompous pills that day and arrogantly dismissed the arrogance of anyone (Dale *who?!*) who would advance such a notion. The fact that many of the gnomic utterances stayed with me, and over the years revealed themselves to be absolutely on the mark, has been a quiet, steady rebuke to my deep streak of hubris.

Happily, Thomajan didn't write me off as brusquely in return. A decade-and-then-some later, when I was settling in to edit my first issue of *Film Comment* magazine (March–April 1990), another envelope was dropped onto my desk. "'Ready When You Are, Mr. Ulmer': Ten Apocryphal Hollywood Tales and What Really Happened" was just the sort of thing I was looking for to help define the "new" *Film Comment* (really a return to the spirit of the great, Richard Corliss-edited *Film Comment* of the 1970s). In it, Thomajan invoked some of the fondest bits of Old Hollywood lore—what Hepburn said upon meeting Tracy, how Orson Welles sized up RKO studios as the "biggest electric train any boy ever had," Hitchcock's assurances to Ingrid Bergman that "it's only a movie"—and proceeded to put his own droll spin on them. I have resolved not to trump the gems in *From Cyd Charisse to* Psycho by quoting too many in advance, so indulge me while I recall my favorite entry from "Ulmer":

The front office learns that John Ford's new movie is two days behind schedule. A flunky is sent down to the set to tell Ford to hurry things up. Ford listens to the complaint, tears ten pages out of the script, and tells the flunky, "There, now I'm back on schedule."

What really happened is this: It had been discovered that, due to faulty mimeographing, several pages of the script appeared in duplicate. When a man from the front office advised Ford of this, Ford tore out the duplicate pages and thanked the man for the information. Standing some thirty feet away was a small boy who was visiting the set that day. The youngster witnessed the incident but couldn't quite make out what was being said. That boy grew up to be Peter Bogdanovich.

One of the most pointless tasks imaginable is trying to explain why someone should find a joke funny, but I can tell you why that story—and Dale Thomajan—is good. The most crucial point of the jest is that movies, their history, the people who make them and *their* history, and the history of the people who watch movies and get ideas about movies and write to share those ideas, all matter. And life in the twentieth century is richer, and infinitely sweeter, if you know that.

Dale Thomajan matters because he knows that. And because he writes gloriously well, with much love and without pretension, false rhetoric, or a wasted word. He has a memory longer than the latest Oscar season and (I am sure) doesn't give a damn about tracking box-office grosses or who's-hot-and-who's-not. And he is possessed of extraordinary good sense—native intelligence, surely, but honed and deepened by a lifetime of experience, moviegoing and otherwise—that both equips and spurs him to say such sensible things about movies. Things so lucid and piercing they immediately come to seem matter-of-fact and invite the reader to self-flatter: that's exactly what I would have said, and indeed was just about to.

"If Pagnol's films are uncinematic (whatever that means), let us not reject Pagnol but instead expand our definition of cinema"; George "Stevens didn't shoot movies, he built them"; re: the rep-house condescension toward Busby Berkeley sequences, "As attitudes of audiences toward art go, I think I prefer vandalism"; on the Korda-Wells *The Man Who Could Work Miracles* as The Best Science-Fiction Movie, "The whole thing is set in a quiet English town in the mid-1930s . . . a time and a place as remote from the futuristic Armageddons of current sci-fi as a blush is from a rash."

There, I've started breaking my resolution—stop me before I quote again! I'll just add that (naturally) I don't always agree with the bestness of the Bests that follow: *my* Best "Hitchcock Movie" Not Directed by Hitchock is Launder & Gilliat's *The State Secret*, and yes of course John Wayne *is* the Best Western Star (although I am mollified by the way

Dale admiringly disqualifies him). I haven't seen *Les Enfants Terribles*, Dale's choice as Best Movie of All Time; I have something to look forward to. And, holding this book open at only page xviii, so do you.

—RICHARD T. JAMESON

★

INTRODUCTION

★

John Wayne was not the best Western movie star; *Gone With the Wind* was not the best three-hour film; and Spencer Tracy was not Hollywood's best actor. To find out who and what actually were, read on.

This is a book of movie "bests." It is not, however, a reference book; it's a book of opinions, my opinions—and it's quite possible that *my* best will not always correspond to *your* best or *the* best. In other words, this book was written not to settle arguments but to start them. Please feel free, therefore, to second-guess it, sass it, or even to bounce it off a wall or two if you wish.

If, on the other hand, it introduces you to the pleasures of just one unfamiliar film, film moment, or film personality, I will be content in the knowledge that my work—to quote Lina Lamont in *Singin' in the Rain*—ain't been in vain fer nothing.

★

|

FILMS

★

★

THE BEST
Love Scene

★

"What Is This Thing Called Love?" is playing softly on the sound track. After a date with her fiancé, Jean Arthur is being walked home by Joel McCrea, one of her roommates; this is wartime Washington and the housing shortage has forced people to double and triple up on living accommodations—hence the movie's title, *The More the Merrier*. The balmy weather and possibly the evening's drinks have made Arthur a little dizzy and as she and McCrea turn the corner of their block, she almost walks into one of the many spooning couples who are lining the sidewalk. So begins a classic screen love scene, one that has never been surpassed in comic-erotic intensity.

You'd never know it from the dialogue. The scene begins with Jean inquiring about Joel's family; he manages to keep up his end of the conversation, if only barely. Meanwhile his hands seem to have acquired a life of their own—they take her arm, they encircle her waist, they keep taking off and then putting on her wrap, somehow managing to come to rest on the wrong side of the wrap in the process. (In addition to the wrap, Arthur is wearing an alluring black lace, off-the-shoulder evening dress, a string of white pearls, and a white flower in her hair.) As the talk progresses from his family to

Joel McCrea and Jean Arthur

his girlfriends, they almost kiss, she pulls away, he absent-mindedly embraces her, and they half-collapse on the front stoop of their apartment building. Arthur and McCrea play the rest of the scene like a pair of strangers who, after falling asleep in a bomb shelter, have awakened in a groping, semi-conscious amorous embrace. She—doing virtually all the talking now—arrives at the subject of marriage, her plans for the future, and her fiancé: "I consider myself a very lucky little lady, being engaged to Mr. Pendergast." She submits her engagement ring for his approval; he kisses her wrist. The legendary Arthur voice is now beginning to break even more than usual as, in large close-up, he nuzzles her neck. "Well, you see," she says distractedly, "that's the way with those older men like Mr. Pendergast. A girl gets to appreciate their more mature"—he finally succeeds in kissing her on the lips—"viewpoint." She pauses and kisses him back—harder. Everything now but their conversation is getting out of hand. Realizing this she politely excuses herself and gets to her feet. "Good night, Mr. Carter," she says. "Good night, Miss Milligan," he says and starts to walk away. Then he remembers where he lives, and both of them enter their building to face what promises to be a very uncomfortable night's sleep.

★

THE BEST
Movie over Three Hours Long

★

Everybody has his or her *Gone With the Wind*; mine is *Giant*. The story of twenty-five years in the life of a rich Texas family, *Giant* was based on a novel by Edna Ferber and directed by George Stevens. Stevens didn't shoot movies, he built them, favoring a slow, brick-by-brick approach to film-making that some have found constrictive, even heavy-handed. When enough ambition, sincerity, and inspiration are added to the formula, however, this kind of cinema, a craftsman's cinema, will occasionally produce a masterpiece like *Giant*. Rarely has one movie yielded so many privileged moments:

- At the dinner table in their stately Maryland home, Leslie Lynnton (Elizabeth Taylor) and her family politely bully embarrassed cattle king Bick Benedict (Rock Hudson) into talking about Texas and his enormous ranch there. ("But come now, Mr. Benedict, can't you be more specific? Well, what's the size of your place?")

- Honeymooners Leslie and Bick travel by rail from the lush, rolling greenery of Maryland into utter Texas desolation, where they finish their trip in an open car, which voraciously bisects an endless expanse of sandy brown nothingness to arrive at the Benedict homestead, a box sitting on a desert.

- In one of the movie's most strikingly composed scenes, Bick's hard-as-nails sister, Luz (Mercedes McCambridge) introduces Leslie to the Benedict Reata's most feckless employee (James Dean): "Jett, this is Bick's new wife. Leslie, this boy here is Jett Rink." Jett can't seem to make up his mind whether or not to shake hands.

- After Jett inherits a small piece of the Reata from Luz, Bick and the local Establishment try to buy him off, but Jett decides to "gamble along with old Madama" and keep the property. Dean's very sly and witty manipulation of his body, his drawl, and a weighted rope he's fooling with made this scene an overnight classic.

- Jett paces off the perimeters of his scrubby inheritance, then climbs a windmill to survey his windfall, and the importance of the moment propels Dimitri Tiomkin's stirring score to new heights of excitement and eloquence.

- Set against the umber brocaded wallpaper of the massive Benedict living room, Uncle Bawley Benedict (Chill Wills), the film's spiritual and cultural anchor, talks about Texas as he plays "Clair de Lune" on the organ and Leslie listens.

- Jett strikes oil on his property and celebrates by getting drunk, parking his broken-down pickup on the Benedict front lawn, coming on to Leslie, sucker-punching Bick, and beating a hasty retreat. As Jett's truck disappears in the distance, Uncle Bawley placidly delivers the film's most memorable lines: "Bick, you should have shot that fella a long time ago. Now he's too rich to kill." Intermission.

- It is fifteen years later and the Benedicts are glumly discussing the colossal day-long party their old nemesis Jett Rink is planning to throw for himself in town. Bick decides the Benedicts will buy a high-powered jet plane and travel to the affair in style, and as he mimes the flight of the jet with his arms, we hear a deafening roar and the scene dissolves to a thundering herd of horses being observed by Bick from the window of his new plane.

- Just before the Jett Rink Day dinner begins, while everyone's loading up on cocktails, a magnificent thunderstorm bursts open the windows of the room. Uncle Bawley,

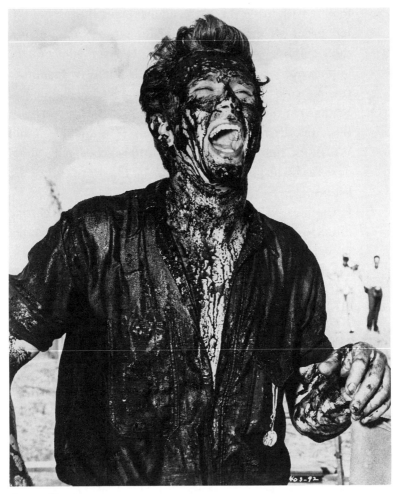

James Dean

waving his arms and bellowing cattle calls, corrals the
delighted guests, excited by the storm and the liquor and
the occasion, and herds them into the banquet room next

door. (For the record, *Giant* contains the most refreshingly affectionate portrait Hollywood has yet painted of America's most severely and unjustly maligned class, the *nouveaux riches*.)

- Bick loses an enthralling, saloon-style brawl in a diner to its proprietor, "Sarge," as the jukebox blares "The Yellow Rose of Texas."

- Back at the homestead, Leslie assures Bick he's not the failure he thinks he is as they sit contemplating the future of Texas and their two grandchildren, one of them Anglo pink, the other Latino brown, and, after three and a quarter hours of bravura filmmaking, Stevens ends his epic, in a moment of great serenity and sweetness, with two enormous, looming close-ups of the children. After the final shot fades to black we are treated to a rousing chorus of "The Eyes of Texas."

Aside from *Giant*'s somewhat paternalistic attitude toward its Mexican characters, the movie is flawed only by a comic scene in which the Benedict children realize that the Thanksgiving turkey they are about to feast on is an old friend from the backyard. When they begin shedding what are apparently real tears, an intrusively naturalistic tone takes over and almost scuttles the movie. (This was not the first time Stevens had shot himself in the foot pandering to the worst tastes of his audience. Following *Swing Time*'s "Pick Yourself Up," one of Fred Astaire's and Ginger Rogers's most captivating numbers, Stevens inserted, or allowed to be inserted, an ugly parody of the number, with Victor Moore and Helen Broderick filling in for Astaire and Rogers. It's a ghastly bit of desperation at a moment when there couldn't be less reason for desperation.)

Giant's three central performances could not have been improved on. James Dean, in his final role, indicates he might have become an outstanding character actor. His older Jett Rink has been criticized for resembling a young man in middle-age makeup, but I feel this is precisely how a rootless man like Jett Rink would look and act as he ages. Much more surprising than Dean's are the intelligent and highly appealing performances of two of Hollywood's most handsome but least talented superstars, Rock Hudson and Liz Taylor, as the boyish, stubborn Bick and the gracious, independent-minded Leslie. As one watches this rather incompatible couple gradually adjust to each other as they grow old—and as the interior of their home evolves from the rich, dark colors of one century to the soft, bland hues of the next—one comes to care deeply for them and for their family, their friends, their way of life, and the land that surrounds them with its harsh poetry.

★

THE BEST
Trailer

★

The first thing we see is a familiar portly figure awaiting us outside a motel as a superimposed legend announces that "the fabulous Mr. Alfred Hitchcock is about to escort you on a tour of the location of his new motion picture, *Psycho*." Which, for the next six minutes, is precisely what happens. As he guides us through the now familiar territory of these grounds, Hitchcock, at various points, starts to tell us disjointed bits of *Psycho*'s story but frequently has to stop in midsentence, appalled by the sordidness of the whole affair. Our tour proceeds from the exterior of the motel to the gloomy old house on the hill (in which, Hitchcock tells us, "the most dire, horrid events took place"), then inside the house to the foot of the stairs ("and in no time the victim tumbled and fell with a *horrible* crash—I think the back broke *immediately* it hit the floor"), then into the master bedroom (where our host opens the door of a wardrobe, looks inside, sees something, turns to the camera, and shudders wordlessly), then back to the motel and inside the small room behind the office (where Hitchcock, pointing to a painting on the wall, declares, "This picture has great significance—*because* . . . ," and leaves it at that).

Ultimately we arrive in the bathroom of Cabin #1. "Well,

they cleaned all this up now," Hitchcock observes. "Big difference. You should have seen the blood. The whole—the whole place was—well, it's too horrible to describe. Dreadful." After lifting the toilet seat to direct our attention to the location of an important clue, Hitchcock gets to the point: "The murderer, you see, crept in here, very slowly, of course, the shower was on, there was no sound . . . and, uh . . ." At this juncture he stops, seemingly hypnotized by something to his off-screen right. After a pause he walks over to the shower and then—with one sudden swipe of his arm—*yanks* the curtain open. Cut to a frontal shot of the head and naked shoulders of a woman,* whose ear-splitting scream is echoed by Bernard Herrmann's shrieking violins as the word PSYCHO, in superimposed white block lettering zooms toward us until it fills the screen. Then the background fades to black and the title breaks into fragments.

---

*It's Vera Miles, not Janet Leigh.

★

THE BEST

Feel-Good Ending in a High School Movie

★

They have nothing in common except likability. She (Ione Skye) is the class brain and beauty, a shy but determined girl whose diligence has won her a major fellowship at an English university. He (John Cusack) is just another guy, a kid with no ambition beyond a vague desire to become a professional kick-boxer ("the sport of the future," he informs her father). Her drive has made her prone to apprehensiveness; his lack of it has made him courageous in an easygoing way. He makes her laugh; she makes him want to cry. He teaches her how to drive; she makes love to him in the back seat. The movie is Cameron Crowe's comedy-drama-romance *Say Anything.*

It is the summer after graduation. He has just told her father that he intends to accompany her to England and look after her there: "What I really want to do with my life, what I want to do for a living—I want to be with your daughter. I'm good at it." Two scenes later we see two pairs of hands clutching. Cut to an angled shot of boy and girl seated side by side; their flight to England is about to depart and she's deathly afraid of flying. "It's like a big roller coaster," he assures her. "Everybody likes roller coasters, right?" She manages a tiny nod. The plane starts to vibrate; it's taking off. "All right—high-level airline safety tips," he says. "If anything happens it usually happens in the first five minutes of the flight." "OK," she says, as bravely as she can. He points upward. "So when you hear that smoking sign go ding you know everything's going to be OK." "OK." Her eyes are glued to the smoking sign. He continues to comfort her. She kisses him hard and says, "Nobody thought we'd do this. Nobody really thinks it will work, do they?" "No. You just described every great success story." He puts his arm around her. A shot from their point of view of the NO SMOKING/ FASTEN SEAT BELT sign, still lit. A straight-on shot of them staring upward at it. "Where's the ding?" she asks anxiously. "It's coming. Any second now." A very extended shot of them looking up, then at each other, then up again. "Any second now," he says and hugs her a little tighter. A long pause, and then a sound.

"Ding." Cut to black.

★

THE BEST
Chaplin Short

★

Charlie Chaplin is so closely associated with the Little Tramp that it's easy to forget he had another great character in his repertoire: a rich, usually inebriated playboy in whom Chaplin combined the dexterity of Nijinski with the stoned insouciance of Reggie van Gleason the Third. No one has ever played a funnier drunk than Chaplin; he could feign lack of control with wondrous control and he had a knack of appearing to unfocus his eyes that was uncanny—at times you can almost see tiny comic-strip circles in front of them.

"One A.M." was the sixth of ten films Chaplin made in 1916. An acrobatic enactment of a *bon vivant*'s return to his homestead after a long wet night on the town, the movie is divided into four movements: "Getting Out of the Cab," "Getting Into the House," "Getting Up the Stairs," and "Getting Into Bed." After Charlie grapples for a couple of minutes with a recalcitrant cab door, the cabby drives off, leaving the rest of the movie to Chaplin, who proceeds to perform a remarkable tour de force of nonstop solo slapstick interrupted only by a few expendable intertitles. Most of the action unfolds in the downstairs interior of Charlie's house, a classic oddball set eccentrically furnished with a menagerie of sinister stuffed animals and dominated by two steep staircases

15

Charlie Chaplin

that lead up to and flank a second-story landing sentineled by a giant swinging pendulum.

There are more than fifty distinct laughs in this gag-packed two-reeler; here are a few of the most inspired.

1. Confronted with a stuffed wildcat, Charlie kicks the beast in its hindquarters causing it to spin and bite him on the leg in a miraculously timed gag that sends him spats over teakettle.

2. A donkey-and-carrot situation arises when Charlie, his cape snagged on the edge of a revolving circular table, tries to lay hold of a decanter of wine sitting on the table's diametrically opposite edge.

3. In his fifth attempt to scale the thirteen-step flight of stairs leading to the second floor, Charlie makes it almost to the top before losing his footing and toppling all the way back down, cocooning himself in the stairway carpeting as he goes.

4. Charlie leaps on a wall-bed that won't stay put* and he falls through its frame, which immediately reverts to its alcove in the wall leaving Charlie and his bedding alone on the floor; then, as Charlie gets to his feet, the bed frame descends again, just in time to give him something to trip over. (Charlie concludes the sequence and the movie by settling in for the night in his bathtub.)

---

*"The funniest and most perverse Murphy bed in movie history."—James Agee.

★

THE BEST

MGM Musical Not to Involve Fred Astaire, Judy Garland, Gene Kelly, or Vincente Minnelli

★

Unlike, say, the Tragedy of the Unwed Mother, the College Musical is not one of those movie genres that became passé with changing times and mores—it was ridiculous right from its inception. All the more surprising that *Good News* proved to be such very good news for 1947 moviegoers. Based on a 1927 Broadway show, *Good News* was filmed twice by MGM—once in 1930 (in a version that still exists, though someone seems to have misplaced the ending) and again seventeen years later, this time in dazzling '40s Technicolor. The latter version's credits were not that promising. Charles Walters had never directed a film before. June Allyson was an acquired taste (one I guarantee you'll acquire once you've seen *Good News*). And Peter Lawford? Singing and dancing? Who could have predicted that *Good News* would be so terrific—that every number would turn out to be a genuine classic of songwriting, musical arrangement, staging, and performance? Starting right off with the title song, which sets us down on the campus of Tait College as a chorus of students are singing its praises in an infectious routine built around basic cheerleading formations and chants—all of this presided over by Joan McCracken, a peppy little dancer-actress whom James Agee likened to "a libidinous peanut."

Next, football hero Peter Lawford educates scrawny scrub Ray McDonald in how to "Be a Ladies' Man"—said seminar beginning in the boys' locker room and evolving across miles it seems of lush and lovely green campus until ultimately both master and apprentice ladykiller take a perfectly timed flying somersault over a four-foot hedge and come up shaking hands. A sensational song-and-dance number.

"Lucky in Love" is one of the most clever and appealing examples of serial ensemble singing you'll ever see and hear. Set in and around a sorority house during a mixer, the number utilizes everyone in the cast who can sing and one or two who can't: in order of appearance, 1. Patricia Marshall (singing to rich-man-on-campus Robert Strickland), 2. Joan McCracken (singing to official boyfriend Loren Tindall and secret squeeze Ray McDonald), 3. the chorus, 4. Mel Tormé (singing to a cute coed), 5. June Allyson (singing to a stack of dishes she's doing), 6. the chorus, 7. Peter Lawford (singing to whoever cares to listen), 8. the chorus (singing to Lawford), and, finally, 9. Mel Tormé again (singing to nobody in particular).

Next, student librarian Allyson gives flunking jock Lawford an accelerated "French Lesson" that was immediately ac-

June Allyson, Peter Lawford, Patricia Marshall, Ray McDonald, and Joan McCracken

claimed as an awesome tour de force of linguistic tongue-twisting.

In the plaza outside the library, girl sings boy the film's most beloved number, "The Best Things in Life Are Free." June sings it less than perfectly and more than wonderfully and looks beautiful doing it. Peter, who moments before had flirted a bit with June during "The French Lesson," is now falling in love with her. Later on he'll sing "Best Things" back to her—in French!

McCracken urges McDonald and an assortment of Tait coeds and eddies to "Pass That Peace Pipe," a novelty song with another tongue-twisting lyric, this one incorporating a hypnotically rhythmic litany of every imaginable (and some imaginary) North American Indian tribe whose name begins with *Ch*. All takes place in the campus malt shop and climaxes in the mock-torrid tom-tom-foolery of a pseudonative mating dance. Four-and-a-half minutes of great fun, this would be a showstopper in a lesser musical.

"Just Imagine" (well, maybe *every* number isn't a genuine classic), in which June, having been (figuratively) seduced and (literally) abandoned, just imagines what things would be like were not Peter such a heartless cad.

The big school dance. June instructs Peter and dozens of black-tied boys and pastel-gowned girls in the ups and downs of "The Varsity Drag" and it's a treat from beginning to end. The dancing here seems to be executed as much with arms as with legs (lots of synchronized semaphoring) and there's a nice bit that combines the formality of a reception line with square-dance elements and chorus-girl kicks. All ultimately segues into an unexpected reprise of "The French Lesson" with the cast forming a human wedding cake as the camera tracks in over the bottom layer (the chorus), then up to a second tier (Tindall, Marshall, McCracken, and McDonald), and higher still to pre–bride-and-groom June and Peter who kiss, steal a peek at the camera to see if they're being observed, discover they are, and then decide, what the hell, to kiss again as the movie ends. In 1947 one wept in dumb joy. One still does.

★

THE BEST
Stylized Dialogue

★

Based on a scorching Ernest Lehman novelette about the Broadway publicity jungle, *Sweet Smell of Success*, a 1957 movie of enormous wit, juice, and power, teamed Burt Lancaster (superb), as J.J. Hunsecker, a manipulative and egomaniacal gossip columnist, with the young, sleekly handsome Tony Curtis (even better), as Sidney Falco, a frantically ambitious press agent. (The casting of Curtis, considered at the time little more than a male starlet, was responsible, I assume, for the various references to Falco as "Eyelashes" and "the boy with the ice cream face.") Drafted to spice up Lehman's screenplay was Clifford Odets, a writer whose distinctive flair for dialogue contributed immeasurably to what became and remains one of the most pungently worded scripts of all time—a heady compound of poeticized gutter lingo, Biblical rhythms, Yiddish phrase inversion, and hard-guy metaphor. Here is a sampling:

J.J. to Sidney, regarding a commitment Sidney has failed to honor: "Sidney, conjugate me a verb—for instance, to promise." Sidney to his uncle, a theatrical agent: "You're walking around blind, Frank, without a cane," and later to J.J.: "You're blind, Mr. Magoo." Uncle Frank (Sam Levene) to a client: "If he offers you an olive branch, so today like olives." J.J. to Sidney: "You sound happy, Sidney. Why should you be happy when I'm not?" Sidney to J.J.: "J.J., peace on earth and good will to men—everything's working out the way I planned." J.J. to Sidney: "I'd hate to take a bite out of you—you're a cookie full of arsenic" and "Sidney, this syrup you're giving out with, you pour over waffles, not J.J. Hunsecker." Brute cop Harry Kello (Emile Meyer), after Sidney has zapped him with a parting insult: "Come back, Sidney, I want to chastise you." And—get this—Sidney, about to impart his philosophy of life to his secretary: "My experience I can give you in a nutshell and I didn't dream it in a dream either." Wow!

People don't actually talk like this, of course—even in the movies; heightened dialogue is very difficult to write, particularly for use in an ostensibly naturalistic film such as *Sweet Smell of Success*. Few screenwriters even attempt this kind of thing (Adrien Joyce's beautiful dialogue for *The Shooting* is one of the rare exceptions). It's a tribute to the audacity of *Sweet Smell of Success*'s writers, cast, and director, Alexander Mackendrick, that they managed to bring it off and did so with such brilliance.

Attention movie oddity sleuths and collectors: Somewhere there's a print of *Sweet Smell of Success* minus much of its magnificent score (the result, my guess is, of an attribution dispute between Elmer Bernstein and Chico Hamilton). I don't remember when or where I saw this deformed print, but I swear I saw it somewhere—and I didn't dream it in a dream either.

★

THE BEST

Movie Composed Entirely of a Single Shot

★

The equivalent of a music video shot in the Garden of Eden before the fall or even the advent of Adam and Eve, Bruce Baillie's *All My Life* lasts exactly as long as it takes Ella Fitzgerald (backed up by Teddy Wilson and his Orchestra) to sing the song of the same name that accompanies it. The film is essentially a slow, westward pan along the face of a weather-beaten and irregularly slatted picket fence interrupted here and there by gaps and dense clusters of small red flowers. Below the fence is long, waving grass; above it is clear blue sky; beyond it is—who knows?—maybe the ocean. After about one hundred feet the camera picks up a diagonally strung telephone wire that it follows northeast until the fence drops out of range, then the wire drops out of range, and the movie ends in pure blue. During its quarter-century of existence, *All My Life* has become a little tarnished and discolored, but Bruce Baillie's tattered Valentine is still one of the cinema's most precious miniatures.

★

THE BEST
Sports Movie

★

Best all-time entry in a very fallow field, the sports movie, would be *Body and Soul*, were boxing a sport. Football, on the other hand, does qualify as a sport, if only barely, because the efforts of its participants to beat the bejesus out of each other have been legitimized by the proximity of a token ball. My selection for best sports movie is *North Dallas Forty*, an honest, intelligent, mildly daring, and highly entertaining examination of a typical pro football team and its players, coaches, owners, and hangers-on. Here we have football not as it was played by Harold Lloyd and Peter Lawford but as it's played today—in an era when "winning isn't everything, it's the only thing" (to quote Vince Lombardi's unfortunately famous non sequitur), when computers are replacing coaches, and when players tend to fall into one of two opposite but equally puerile camps: absurdly naive Christians or half-crazed, brute pagans. Miles from the former but still safely short of the latter is our hero Phil Elliot, veteran wide receiver, team clown, and his own man—or so he thinks. We first encounter Phil after a pill-and-pilsner breakfast, tweezing wads of bloody cotton out of his nostrils—it seems he's a member not only of the North Dallas Bulls but also of the walking wounded, thanks to too many seasons in the ranks of America's favorite contact sport. The movie's classic theme is stated in the following first-reel exchange between Elliot and starting Bulls quarterback Seth Maxwell. Elliot: "If you start pretending to be somebody else, that's what you're gonna end up being, somebody else." Maxwell: "I'm gonna tell you something for your own good. You had *better* learn how to play the game—and I don't just mean the game of football." Maxwell, of course, is talking about the game of survival, the one most of us have to play every day to stay afloat. What he knows and Elliot is about to find out is that giving one hundred percent on the field (an honest day's work for an honest day's pay) just isn't enough; like Edward G. Robinson in *Key Largo*, the men with all the marbles want "more." Elliot, as Bulls brass and coaches repeatedly remind him, is guilty of "individualism," a dangerously anachronistic sin in an age when "team effort" is holy writ. (In truth, the Bulls are merely looking for an excuse to dump him in favor of a younger player.) Elliot ultimately discovers that the powers-that-be are themselves secret subscribers to the heresy of individualism and that the only individuals they care about are themselves. As he puts it in his climactic confrontation with "The Man": "*We're* not the team [referring to the players and coaches] . . . *They're* the team [pointing to the owners] . . . *We're* the equipment." If all this isn't exactly news to anyone who's ever worked for wages, it's a pleasure to see *North Dallas Forty* restate it so skillfully and eloquently. Perhaps even more impressive and certainly more unusual is the movie's hard-nosed portrayal of the day-to-day pressures and pains pro ballplayers suffer—a portrayal that peaks in *North Dallas Forty*'s most accomplished sequence: a Monday night game in Chicago, plotted in three scenes. Scene 1 is a minutely detailed anthology of the many and various pregame, locker-room rituals players enact to get themselves up (or in some cases down) for a game. Scene 2 is devoted to the climax of the contest itself (and it's all quite exciting—football *is*, after all, a pretty good game). Scene 3 returns us to the locker room where a linesman (played by ex-pro John Matuszak) bursts into an unexpected and impassioned protest against the players' status as high-income serfs, a refrain that Elliot will reprise with only a bit less emotion a couple of scenes later.

North Dallas Forty is not nearly as heavy as I've made it sound; high jinks, humor, and some wickedly amusing dialogue are a large part of the package. In the film's funniest line, for example, Elliot suggests a sign for the prospective restaurant of a particularly barbaric teammate: "Joe Bob's Fine Foods—Eat Here or I'll Kill You." Bo Svenson, by the way, gives a very strong performance as Joe Bob. Not surprisingly, Nick Nolte, arguably today's finest film actor, is toweringly sympathetic as Phil Elliot. Quite surprising, on the other hand, is country singer Mac Davis's fetching and totally convincing portrayal of Maxwell, a Machiavellian good-old-boy who long ago learned the rules of the game.

Warning: Do not walk out of, switch off, or rewind *North Dallas Forty* prematurely. A priceless cinematic paradiddle emerges in the film's final two shots when Davis, Nolte, and a football combine to bring the movie's central metaphor brilliantly and literally to life.

★

THE BEST

(Feature) Comedy
under Seventy Minutes Long

★

Like their stars, movies of the early 1930s tended to be blunt, tough, and short. It wasn't that the plots of these celluloid-skimpers were especially sparse—you usually were given a full ninety minutes of plot, but you got it on less than seventy-five minutes of film. This feat was accomplished through a combination of split-second transitions, dizzying montages, and frenetic line readings by superenergized actors playing characters who always seemed to be running late. Warner Bros. films in particular appear to have operated under the general principle that both their casts and their audiences were anxious to get on with it so that everybody could get to the track.

Jimmy the Gent is an excellent example of early Warner fare, a sixty-seven-minute razzle-dazzler based on the questionable premise that not only are there people who make their livings solely by discovering or, if honesty fails, creating heirs to unclaimed fortunes but that there's an entire heir-hunting industry out there—complete with elaborate offices, competing firms, corporate spying, and so on. The film's title character, played by James Cagney, is introduced through a close-up of the back of his haircut, a sort of a Stone Age fade broken up with a bottle scar here, a dangerously throbbing vein there. James Corrigan, so named possibly because he does everything the wrong way, is a rough-and-ready fella whose heir-chasing racket has brought him riches but not, he realizes, the two things he craves most: Joan Martin, a feisty former assistant who's defected to his chief rival, James J. Wallingham, and class, an amorphous attribute symbolized to Corrigan by the tea that is perpetually being served in Wallingham's offices. Corrigan's hilarious attempts to acquire both the girl and the graces are the foundations for one of Cagney's most audacious performances. Gone is most of the trademark menace, the cute-customer craftiness, the mock-effeminacy, the awesome bits of sudden dancelike activity— all is sacrificed to pure and single-minded, bullheaded, forward-tilting propulsion or, in a word, *thrust*. It may be a one-note performance, but it's a high note. Supporting Cagney, along with Warner's usual assortment of morons and milksops, are a pair of nifty blondes:* Bette Davis, still in her bearable period, and Alice White, marvelously daffy as a cute trick who's so dim she doesn't even know she's a doxy. *Jimmy the Gent*'s lingo frequently rises (or descends) to the level of its characters: "*f* like in *finagle*"; "superannuated spinster"; "Louie looks up birt'marks," a job description; "She ate a poisoned cheese sandwich and turned up her toes"; "Sufficientuntothedayistheevilthereof," Cagney quoting from Matthew 6:34 in under two seconds; a retreating Cagney to Arthur Hohl regarding Alice White—"Cope with that for a minute, willya?"; a retreating Davis as she is extricating herself from

Blondes and Bonds was one of *Jimmy the Gent*'s working titles.

Wallingham's advances—"I need a haircut"; and most memorably, in one of the great classic lines of the period, nouveaugent Jimmy to brand-new butler as Davis looks on—"You can serve tea and screw, Arlington."

★

THE BEST
Movie Moment

★

Harry Lime is killed in a traffic mishap shortly before *The Third Man* begins. Holly Martins (Joseph Cotten), unconvinced his friend's death was accidental, is investigating the matter in his own bumbling way. It is late in the movie and late at night in a dark, deserted square when the mewing of a cat alerts Martins, who is alone and a little drunk, that a man in a nearby doorway is spying on him. All Martins can make out are the spy's shoes, an expensive pair of highly polished wing tips, and, nestling between them, the telltale cat—the rest of the doorway is in shadow. Martins challenges the man to step out into the open. No response. Eventually Martins' voice awakens a woman in an adjacent apartment who turns on her lights, illuminating the upper portion of the spy's hiding place. As the camera slowly travels forward and the film's zither score breaks into its signature melody, we see the face of Orson Welles, lit as if by a

theater pin spot. As though sharing a joke with the man confront-
ing him and with his old friends in the audience, Welles smiles
and lightly pokes his cheek with his tongue. Instantly an intoxicating aura of mischief, wit, and intrigue seizes the movie and
elevates it to a new level of sophistication. "Harry!" says Martins.

★

THE BEST
"Woman's Picture"

★

The "woman's picture" was a staple of Hollywood's golden
age. A drama or melodrama about man's inhumanity to
woman, a woman's picture centers on a female character
(usually played by a major star) who is driven to or over the
brink by the selfishness or weakness of a male character (often
played by a second-string matinee-idol type) whose own
needs and problems are represented as so inconsequential,
except as plot devices, that his name might as well be
McGuffin. By tradition, woman's pictures are so frequently
and so deeply rooted in self-pity, self-sacrifice, and self-
absorption that, in my opinion, taken as a genre they ought
to be called "Self Cinema." There are, of course, many
exceptions—the most gratifying being an early Ingmar Bergman film called *Summer Interlude* (or sometimes *Illicit Inter-*

lude). Bergman didn't stoop to ennobling his protagonist by making the man she loves contrastingly ignoble—the only sin *Summer Interlude*'s main man commits is dying in his midteens. Thirteen years later we find our heroine, now an aging ballerina of twenty-eight, unable and, worse, unwilling to shake off the tragedy of her adolescent sweetheart's death and free her soul from sorrow. Even the attentions of the handsome and refreshingly down-to-earth reporter with whom she is having a halfhearted affair fail to reverse her retreat from life or penetrate her shell of misery. One day, on an impulse, she ferries back to the island of her youth where she relives in her mind the two-month idyll she shared there with her doomed young lover. ("The days were like shining pearls on a thread of gold, overflowing with fun and caresses. Nights of wide-awake dreams. When did we sleep?") That night, back on the mainland, alone in her dressing room "with neither the courage to live nor to die," she looks in the mirror and a miracle happens. . . . A few years later Bergman would run a similar reverse to conclude *The Magician*, but *Summer Interlude*'s climactic epiphany is even more satisfying because it is even less justified. (The average professor of screenwriting, a notoriously secular craft, would scrawl "motivation?" in the margins of *Summer Interlude*'s final pages.)

Summer Interlude is not only one of Bergman's most accessible works, it's one of his most haunting. A slow, melancholy greasepaint-and-soap opera that ultimately overwhelms one with its evocative blending of landscapes, still lifes, faces, and metaphor, it's a "tearjerker" one can respond to without feeling like a jerk. Why then is it not regarded highly as a woman's film, or even as a Bergman film? In a 1975 poll seven

Maj-Britt Nilsson and Birger Malmsten

prominent female filmmakers and writers were asked individually to name the ten best films about women. None of them cited *Summer Interlude*, though one had the nerve to list *Last Tango in Paris*; and another, *Bonnie and Clyde*. What ten films would *I* have chosen? I thought you'd never ask.

Ella Cinders (1926)
The Wind (1928)
Mannequin (1937)
Black Narcissus (1947)
Summer Interlude (1951)
Nights of Cabiria (1957)
Mouchette (1966)

Isabel (1968)
The Grasshopper (1970)
The Story of Adele H. (1975)

★

THE BEST
Two-Character Movie

★

John Boorman followed his 1967 classic *Point Blank* with a fascinating tale of two Second World War soldiers, an American and a Japanese, struggling to survive on a small deserted island, first at each other's expense and later with each other's cooperation. As the cast consists only of Lee Marvin and Toshiro Mifune, two of the most kinetic actors in the history of talkies, and as neither speaks the other's language, the story is as much danced as it is acted. Marvin in particular is physically eloquent; he combines the lame, loping trot of Walter Brennan and the mincing craftiness of Bob Hope with his own uniquely sensuous bodily rhythms in a performance that bounces back and forth between long-shot broadness and close-up subtlety with Chaplinesque ease. The film is an allegory, as its title suggests, and the allegory is tolerable, but it's on the level of pure old-fashioned open-air adventure that *Hell in the Pacific* impresses most (bring the kids; they'll love it). Boorman, an Englishman, has a Japanese talent for integrating his performers with his terrain; seldom in fact has the wide-screen format been used as effectively outdoors as it was here. So unless you can find a letter-boxed video, don't even consider renting *Hell in the Pacific*; in the scanned-for-TV format, it simply doesn't work.

★

THE BEST
Movie Cited in the Book
The Fifty Worst Films of All Time

★

Fifteen years ago, during a rainy spring break, two kids wrote a book in which they selected and savaged "the fifty worst films of all time." Although I rather disapproved of the books' concept, I read it anyway, hoping for a few surprises. The surprises were indeed few; instead of roasting such overstuffed sacred turkeys as *Last Tango in Paris* or cult fiascoes like *Harold and Maude*, the book (which, unfortunately, was published shortly before *Apocalypse Now* and *Interiors* were unleashed on an unarmed populace) chose to concentrate mainly on the standard stinkers: *Santa Claus Conquers the Martians*, *The Horror of Party Beach*, *The Terror of Tiny Town*, etc.—strictly minor-league stuff. Nor did the book even afford me much opportunity to wallow in the perverse pleasure of righteous indignation—only three of my pet pictures were included in the foul fifty and two of them, *Ivan the Terrible* and *Last Year at Marienbad*, were overdue for a little kidding. No, only one citation ticked me off: Sam Peckinpah's *Bring Me the Head of Alfredo Garcia*, a move the two "fifty-worst" fellas called "an ultra-violent and meaningless exercise in exploitation and bad taste" and I call one of the few genuinely great films to have emerged from Hollywood since the collapse of the studio system in the late 1950s. Granted, *Alfredo Garcia* is not as polished as most films by Sam Peckinpah, who was a superb craftsman as well as a major artist; the immaculate editing and the relentlessly apt rhythms we had come to expect from him falter at times and the color is so-so, but don't let the rough edges fool you—this movie is a masterpiece. It was first and foremost, I strongly suspect, an attempt by Peckinpah to respond to the charges of gratuitous violence he'd been pelted with ever since he killed off all those extras in *The Wild Bunch*. Peckinpah didn't rebut his critics by eschewing violence in *Alfredo Garcia*—he had already taken that route in his greatest film, *Junior Bonner*—but by marrying the violence to intense pain and anguish, as if to say "There—at least those @#$%¢&*s can't accuse me of *gratuitous* violence anymore." (They could, off course, and they did.)

When a rich and powerful Mexican businessman learns that his young, unmarried daughter is pregnant, he puts a price on the head of the culprit, Alfredo Garcia—cash on delivery of the head. Bennie (Warren Oates), an acquaintance of Garcia's, gets wind of the offer and decides to collect the bounty—which should be a cinch, he figures, because he happens to know that Garcia has died recently and that Bennie's girl, Elita, a singer(?) in a brothel, knows where the body is buried. For the price of a spade and a sword, Bennie's assured of a $10,000 ticket out of his dead-end job as Mexico City's least talented saloon singer-pianist, and into wherever it is Americans who are down on their luck go to change it. (An amusing note of irony is struck when someone jokingly introduces himself to Bennie as "Fred C. Dobbs" and Bennie doesn't seem to get the joke.) And so Bennie, "a neo-knight in quest of an unholy grail,"* packs a shovel and a machete, some food and drink, and Elita into his beat-up Impala and hits the road in search of a head, and a head start on a new life. Along the way to attaining everything he wants in the world, Bennie loses everything he has in the world.

Warren Oates, possibly the finest film actor of the 1970s and probably the most underrated, is Bennie, a little guy who looks like a Mad Comics character drawn by Wally Wood—he's practically all teeth, and what isn't teeth is wardrobe, the latter tending to bargain-basement print shirts with clip-on ties in clashing patterns, and brown-black sunglasses with the opacity of a limousine window. Elita is movingly played by maturing Mexican screen goddess Isela Vega, whose beguiling beauty is best described in the face-of-an-angel/body-of-a-devil vocabulary of pulp fiction blurbs. Robert Webber and Gig Young, as matching hit men with slick fronts and dead

* Scott Mugford

souls, are cult villains second and third to none. Webber, shortly after we meet him, knocks an oversolicitous bar girl unconscious with a single swipe of his elbow, an act so brutal and unexpected it's almost (but not quite) funny. All *Young* has to do to make your heart stop is smile (even *The Fifty Worst Films* authors acknowledged his chilling performance). But the ultimate star of the movie is Sam Peckinpah. In the same way that his hero, Bennie, decides to go all the way with his mad crusade, Peckinpah decided to do likewise with his most emotionally challenging movie; by the time it's over, you know you've seen something. Not our resolute critics though—all they saw was "another line-'em-up-shoot-'em-down-but-in-slow-motion pseudo-Western . . . [with] no point, no sense, and no sensibility." But I forgive them. I can see how the story of two aging whores desperately seeking a second chance might be pointless to a couple of middle-class hotshots with a combined age of thirty-six.

The following is taken from an interview Warren Oates gave in 1980, six years after the release of *Bring Me the Head of Alfredo Garcia*: "Right now Sam's up in Montana. We share a place—it's our heaven. I ran into it four or five years ago; we'd always dreamed of this little ranch somewhere, and now, this year, he came in on it with me. He's built himself a beautiful house, lovely old log place, waaay in the back—it's four-and-a-half miles from the front of my property to the back, and he's in the back, the very back. He's in heaven. And he's going to find solace there, and he's going to start writing, and putting down all of his fury. Something incredible is going to come out of it. I know. Something incredible." Neither Peckinpah nor Oates, however, were to make another great movie, together or apart; four years later they were both dead, and their deaths went as undermourned as their careers had been undervalued.

★

THE BEST
Busby Berkeley Number

★

No one ever created musical numbers like Busby Berkeley's, because no one, with the possible exception of a few animators of the early sound era, has had a mind that worked like his; his extravaganzas are like the imaginings of children just about to fall asleep. Berkeley's childish genius made him a pioneer target of camp condescension and that's why one cannot comfortably watch Berkeley in a revival house; the derisive laughter of the educated audiences who frequent such theaters invariably spoils the fun for the rest of us (the ignorant peasantry). As attitudes of audience toward art go, I think I prefer vandalism.

Berkeley's supreme accomplishment was the marathon "Lullaby of Broadway" number from *Gold Diggers of 1935*. "Lullaby" opens on a black frame interrupted only by the tiny pin-lit face of Winifred Shaw at top center. During the next two minutes, as Wini sings the jaunty-sweet "Lullaby," her face gradually expands until it fills the entire screen, then turns upside down and metamorphoses into a cityscape. A series of mock aerial shots draws us down into the city, where we are about to witness a hauntingly surreal minidrama in the form of a Jazz Age lullaby. This story, a dream within a dream, is told through a dizzying display of cinematic artificiality: tilted shots, gauzy shots, low-angle shots, overhead shots, reverse overhead shots, you name it. All begins at 6:27 A.M. with the long Germanic shadow of a cop walking his lonely morning beat. Then the city comes to life as dairies hum with activity, people awaken, and pretty girls dress for work (a shot of one of them hooking up her bra indicates that *Gold Diggers of 1935* must have only just made it under the wire strung up by Hollywood's prudish Production Code of 1934). Wage earners are now hustling to work, and the cranking of an office pencil sharpener is rhymed with that of an organ-grinder who is heralding the return home of Wini Shaw, escorted by Dick Powell, after a long night out on the town. As Wini climbs the stairs to her flat, a mailman, a cleaning lady, and a couple of work-bound neighbors bid her good night in song. Waiting at her door is her cat, which she feeds with freshly delivered milk; then she rolls down her hose and goes to bed. Twelve hours later she's up and ready to do the town again. Dick picks her up in a cab and after a little backseat petting and club hopping they wind up at the Club Royal where they do some serious drinking in appropriately tilted shots. (When was the last time this couple ate?) Cut to a white-costumed Spanish dance team making its way down a wide, winding flight of stairs and on to a mammoth dance

Wini Shaw, Dick Powell, and dancers

floor broken up into assorted tiers of stairs. As Wini and Dick
look down like monarchs from a table on high, the female
Spanish dancer leads onto the floor an army of pale, blond tap
dancers clad fetchingly and revealingly in black. Meanwhile
her partner has ushered in a similar brigade of dancing boys
and as the two groups merge, the Spanish lady is hoisted up
to plant a quick kiss on Dick who immediately passes it on to
Wini. At this point the girls and boys of the chorus pair off
and break into a spectacular display of mass-synchronized tap.
Everything now is becoming a little weird, if not borderline
sinister: there is no discernible orchestra in this surrealistic

nightclub; there are no patrons other than Wini and Dick; the lighting is a little somber for a temple of gaiety; the exhibition dancing is a touch leaden—is this a dream or a nightmare?

After Wini and Dick do a bit more singing and dancing and smooching, Wini, pursued by Dick and several thousand frenzied dancers, races up to and through a pair of glass doors, which she coquettishly closes behind her. Standing now on a small balcony, she kisses Dick through the glass while the excited mob behind him thrusts forward. The doors swing outward pushing Wini backward over the ledge of the balcony and she falls screaming to the street far below. Then, as the chorus sings "Lullaby" for the last time, we see Wini's bed— empty. Outside the door her cat waits in vain for its morning milk as the camera takes us outside into the city, outward and upward until the city is transformed back into Wini's face, and as she sings the last line of the song, her face recedes to the back of the screen where it began thirteen minutes ago. Finally, we see the audience of Warner Brothers extras who supposedly have been witnessing this musical miracle respond not with derisive laughter but warm applause, and Busby Berkeley's strangest, most fabulous dream is over.

★

THE BEST
Joke in a Credits Sequence

★

In a controversial 1971 essay, Pauline Kael broke the news that Orson Welles actually didn't have all that much to do with *Citizen Kane*, though I'm sure she'd graciously concede that he'd probably seen it. As if in anticipation of his subsequent belittlement, Welles, in a grand moment of false modesty, inserted a priceless little joke in *Kane*'s end credits. Immediately following the story's final images, we are shown a series of shots in which *Kane*'s principal cast members are introduced one by one and allowed to reprise a line or two from the movie—but something is missing: After giving one of the most audacious extended performances in cinema history Orson Welles has apparently missed his curtain call. But wait! On the screen appears a card which lists in small print the cast also-rans: the headwaiter, Mr. Rawlston, Miss Anderson, etc. And there, at the bottom of the heap, eighth line out of eight, right under *Kane, age 8*, is the following credit: *Kane* . . . . ORSON WELLES.

★

THE BEST

Musical in Which Both the Male and Female Stars Are Dancers but Never Dance Together

★

—and probably the only one—*It's Always Fair Weather*, a deft satire on the phony folksiness of TV programming, stars Gene Kelly and Cyd Charisse. Among the movie's many pleasures are Gene dancing with Army buddies Dan Dailey and Michael Kidd, and Gene dancing solo on roller skates—but ever and alas Gene dancing sans Cyd. And when Cyd does a dynamite number, "Baby, You Knock Me Out," with a chorus of pugilistic plug-uglies, Gene is nowhere to be found. According to Hugh Fordin in his book *The World of Entertainment*, Gene and Cyd did dance together to a song called "Love Is Nothing but a Racket," but it was cut from the film before release. So if you're looking for the Charisse-Kelly chemistry (forget *Brigadoon*), look to the big Broadway ballet from *Singin' in the Rain*—the number in which Cyd impales Gene's porkpie hat with one of those legendary legs and lofts it to the heavens.

★

THE BEST
American Independent Movie

★

When *Shadows* was released in 1961 it was hailed as a pioneer work in what everybody hoped would be a domestic New Wave to rival the one then sweeping the French cinema. That golden age of American independent filmmaking never got off the ground, and today, thirty years later, *Shadows* is one of its few watchable legacies. The first movie to be directed by actor John Cassavetes, *Shadows* was based upon acting improvisations Cassavetes had been conducting in his New York drama workshop, and upon a scenario that had evolved from them: the story of a three-sibling, parentless family trying to survive and make it in Manhattan.

Hugh (Hugh Hurd) is an unsuccessful nightclub singer of little discernible talent; his younger half sister, Lelia (Lelia Goldoni), is a beautiful but pretentious, pampered princess; his younger half brother, Benny (Ben Carruthers), is a moody

Rupert Crosse, Hugh Hurd, and Lelia Goldoni

malingerer with a Beat Generation temperament. For a film with the look and reputation of a beatnik classic, *Shadows* has a surprisingly conservative theme: the family—its value, its vulnerability, and its importance, not as a social bulwark (*Shadows* isn't *that* conservative) but as a spiritual necessity. Whether he knows it or not, Hugh is a man with a mission. His continuous and occasionally desperate attempts to hold his relatively unstable family together, and still float a career, make a buck, and maybe even get a life of his own in the process, gradually emerge as noble and cumulatively become positively heroic—one minute he's fighting to keep Benny off the streets and within the family bosom; the next minute he's nursing Lelia through a breakdown following her seduction by a white boy who panicked when he discovered she's a mulatto; in between he's valiantly tendering his art to ill-mannered strip-joint patrons who've come solely to see the girls.

Almost everyone in *Shadows* is hugely sympathetic, in particular: Hugh, the harried knight and unsung saint; Benny, an amusingly petulant punk of great charisma; Lelia, alternately bewitching, exasperating, and heartbreaking; Rupert Crosse, as Hugh's blithe friend and artistic manager; Tom Allen, as one of Benny's Vitelloniesque buddies; and Davey Jones, as Lelia's long-suffering suitor. (Cassavetes himself does not appear in the film except for a cameo in which he emerges from the shadows of 42nd Street's movie-house strip to rescue Lelia from a masher.)

Throughout his directorial career Cassavetes was mischaracterized as a "raw" talent lacking in cinematic aptitude, but to my eye *Shadows* is a very stylish movie. When a filmmaker likes and understands people as deeply as Cassavetes did, art is almost sure to follow; a good illustration of the Cassavetes aesthetic being his use of Ben Carruthers, a curiously handsome, loosey-goosey spider monkey of a presence who instinctively gravitates toward the side or corner of any frame he happens into, creating elegant compositions wherever he goes. In fact there's hardly a frame of *Shadows* I would not be glad to hang on my wall.

A word about improvisation: Improvised dialogue is a bad idea with a long and venerable tradition, but despite the occasional clinker (Benny's line about "that Beat Generation jazz," for example), Cassavetes and the cast of *Shadows* bring it off with great success; like its classic Charlie Mingus score, *Shadows* is funky but not shaggy. That's why I can almost guarantee you that when the movie's end title (and central white lie), *The film you have just seen was an improvisation*, appears on the screen, you will be moved not merely to approve but to applaud.

★

THE BEST
Parody

★

The bogus documentary *All You Need Is Cash* (also known as *The Rutles*) is a lampoon of all those Beatles chronicles that sprang up after the group's breakup and continue to be produced to this day. The story of Dirk, Nasty, Stig, and Barry (a.k.a. the Rutles, a.k.a. "the Pre-Fab Four")—four lads from Liverpool who created in the 1960s "a musical legend that will last a lunchtime"—*Cash* is a fairly gentle and affectionate parody (George Harrison appears in the film as an interviewer) whose satire is generally too broad and deliberately off-the-mark to be malignant; Yoko Ono, for example, is portrayed as a white Aryan Nazi named Chastity. As funny as it is, *Cash*'s true claim to fame is its pseudoauthenticity; no expense was spared in making it look as much like the real thing as possible:* detailed album covers were produced, elaborate "Pathétique" newsreels were shot, and full-blown "film clips" were created in the styles of the Beatles' five feature movies (I'm referring, of course, to *A Hard Day's Rut, Ouch!, Tragical History Tour, Yellow Submarine Sandwich*, and *Let It Rot*). In addition, Neil Innes (who plays Nasty) provided a series of Rutles tunes that not only are redolent of the real Lennon-McCartney McCoy but are quite catchy—though I doubt that "Twist and Rut," "With a Girl Like You," "Get Up and Go," and "I Am the Waitress" are likely to replace the originals in our hearts. At times, indeed, *Cash*'s conceits become almost indistinguishable from what they're spoofing, for instance the following cheeky exchange from a Rutles press conference:

Q. Do you feel better after seeing the Queen?
A. No, you feel better after seeing the doctor.
Q. What are you going to do now?
A. Back to your place.

At other times the humor is pricelessly absurd: An ancient black bluesman being interviewed at the banks of the Mississippi acknowledges that "everything I learned, I learned from the Rutles."

In the process of burlesquing Beatlemania, *All You Need Is Cash* takes a healthy swipe at a bundle of TV-documentary clichés. Eric Idle (who wrote and co-directed the movie, and plays several characters including Dirk) portrays the perennially trench-coated reporter charged with guiding viewers through the appropriate locations ("so we went to New Or-

*At the time of its release (1978), *All You Need Is Cash* was the most costly made-for-TV movie ever produced.

leans to find out just how expensive it is to make these documentaries"); in addition to such minor gaffes as finding himself in the wrong city at the wrong time, Idle has no end of problems with his production crew: On one occasion a runaway camera truck forces him to escalate his perambulatory commentary from a walk to a trot to a desperate gallop.

The movie's last words are spoken by Mick Jagger. When asked if he thinks the Rutles will ever reunite, Jagger replies, "I hope not."

★

THE BEST
Last Line in a Gangster Movie

★

After returning from World War I to find all the good jobs taken, Eddie Bartlett (James Cagney) spends *The Roaring Twenties* working himself up from cabby to successful bootlegger and back down to cabby. Eddie, not a bad mug at heart, is now a three-time loser, having taken it on the chin from the crash of '29, the repeal of Prohibition, and the nice girl he loves, who has married a straight-arrow type who works for the D.A. When he learns that his old cronies from the

Gladys George, James Cagney, and Charles Wilson

rackets are planning to eliminate his ex-girl's husband, Eddie decides to do something constructive for once in his life and wipes them out; in the process he is mortally wounded. His escape from the gangsters' lair leads him to an old cathedral where, after staggering up, down, and across the snow-covered steps for a seeming eternity, he dies in the arms of Panama (Gladys George), the slightly tarnished dame who has loved him in vain. Just after Eddie breathes his last, a cop approaches and asks the grieving Panama who the dead man is. "Eddie Bartlett," she says. "What was his business?" asks the cop. Panama, with equal measures of bitterness and sorrow, replies, "He used to be a big shot."

★

THE BEST

Number in an Otherwise Mediocre Musical

★

Don't hold your breath waiting for MGM's *Ship Ahoy* to hit your favorite video store, movie channel, or repertory cinema; it's fairly lame stuff even by 1942 standards—despite the presence of Bert Lahr, Eleanor Powell, Red Skelton, Virginia O'Brien, the Tommy Dorsey Orchestra, and a very young Frank Sinatra. Midway through this modest black-and-white programmer, however, the Dorsey boys strike up a ca,chy conga as Lahr and Skelton sing about the charms of a certain Tallulah relative to other gals in circulation—and then something wonderful happens. Smartly dressed in turban and whippy skirt, Eleanor Powell swings into action, skipping, kicking, and cartwheeling her way through the poolside area of the luxury liner the film is set on. Tables, chairs, flying rings, even a diving board get into the act as Eleanor serves up two-and-a-half minutes of the most expert and endearing dancing you will ever see. Powell, always an effective hoofer but at times, perhaps, too much the technician, here enters her claim as the cinema's greatest female dancer. Finally, with miraculous precision, she and

Tommy Dorsey, Eleanor Powell, and Red Skelton

Dorseyman Buddy Rich exchange one small drum (thrown), one drumstick (bounced), one handshake (firm), and a pair of smiles (absolutely dazzling)—all this occurring bing-bang-bing in a matter of seconds—then suddenly "I'll Take Tallulah" is over and you find yourself wondering, as you're putting your socks back on, if it all really happened.

★

THE BEST

Visual Gag in a Hitchcock Movie

★

Guy (Farley Granger) and Bruno (Robert Walker) were nothing more than *Strangers on a Train* until Bruno takes it upon himself to murder Guy's shrewish wife. Bruno thinks Guy should return the favor by killing Bruno's father. Guy, with some justification, thinks Bruno has a few toys in the attic. Bruno, however, keeps hounding Guy and on one occasion turns up at a tennis match Guy is participating in. There, Hitchcock captures Bruno's sinister single-mindedness in an audacious shot: Among a sea of sideline spectators, their heads swiveling in concert as they follow the flight of the ball, is one sole swiveless head, its eyes fixed on Guy. It's Bruno's.

★

THE BEST
Moment in a Short

★

Chris Marker's twenty-eight-minute film *La Jetée* is only technically a short; its scenario is substantial enough to easily serve as the basis for a feature-length film. The movie's brevity is the result of an interesting narrative conceit: The story is told, with one exception, entirely through freeze-frames, accompanied by voice-over narration.

A member of a dying community from the postapocalyptic future is sent back to the time and place of his youth in search of survival techniques. During the course of his periodic visits to the past (our present), he meets a young woman and they fall in love. She, not knowing who he is or why he comes and goes so mysteriously, calls him "my ghost." One morning the camera, presumably from the point of view of the protagonist, discovers the young woman in bed, looking, in sleep, very beautiful and serene. All is silence but for the voices, gradually rising in volume, of the morning's birds. A series of shots, dissolving one into the next, record the subtle shiftings of her head and shoulders as she sleeps. Ultimately, barely awake, she appears to blink and almost perhaps half smiles at us— and we realize that we are looking at a "live" shot (it's the film's first and will prove to be its last). To call this shot startling doesn't begin to do justice to the almost supernaturally thrilling beauty of the moment. (Tragically, this fleeting epiphany has become all but imperceptible in *La Jetée*'s murky existing prints. Restoration, anyone?) Shortly thereafter, the film concludes, where it began, on the jetty of Paris's Orly Airport, as the future catches up to the past in one of the most haunting, profound, and staggeringly moving denouements I've ever seen on a movie screen.

★

THE BEST

Canadian Movie

★

Based on Clément Perron's recollections of his childhood, Claude Jutra's *My Uncle Antoine* re-creates a Christmas Eve day (happy) and night (unhappy) in a Quebec country town. The movie is set in and around the town's general store, which is run by a middle-aged couple with the help of a younger clerk and two adolescents, the couple's nephew and an abandoned girl they have taken in. For two-thirds of its length *My Uncle Antoine* is a largely positive portrait of these people, their working-class neighbors, and their milieu. So rich is this film in its detail and so assured in its observation, it never has to rely on sentimentality to warm and win its audience—its very substance is ingratiation enough. Then, in its final half hour, when the flaws in these people and their lives begin to surface, the story turns dark and ultimately devastating.

My Uncle Antoine is one of the great winter films—snow is its stock in trade. Many of the outdoor shots in this handsomely photographed color movie are almost pure black-and-white interrupted only here and there by a faded yellow house or a red Coca-Cola sign. The town's main street has a personality of its own; anyone who grew up in the nonurban north will recognize it and the old, wooden, two- and three-family houses that line it. Among *My Uncle Antoine*'s many other virtues are: an outstanding score executed mainly with violin and accordian; the poignant semisexual, semisiblinglike relationship of the two children; a nice running gag centered on an unusually stolid barrel of nails; a hushed journey by horse and buggy through miles of snow and moonlight; and a rare look from deep inside the bone of an entire society of people whose souls are being worn away by a mean economy, a harsh climate, an austere culture, and something peculiarly, insidiously northern.

★

THE BEST
Line Delivered by a Woman to the Jealous Husband She Is Dumping

★

"From now on, you're the only man in the world that my door is closed to."
—Norma Shearer to Chester Morris in *The Divorcée*

★

THE BEST
High School Movie

★

Over the years the appeal of 20th Century-Fox's *Margie* has expanded from nostalgia for the era it is largely set in, the late 1920s, to include nostalgia for the one in which it was produced, the mid-1940s. The movie begins in the present (1946) with the title character and her teenage daughter rummaging through their attic where they come upon an archaic pair of baggy bloomers. ("Gee, they're *hid*eous," comments Margie, Jr.) Margie's old bloomers move daughter to implore mother to "tell me all about the crazy and idiotic things you did when you were my age." Flash back eighteen years to a then slightly and now irrevocably bygone era when ceilings were high, streets were straight, clothing was woolen, and suburban rot had not yet eroded the foundations of small-town America.

Margie MacDuff is a sixteen-year-old who suffers from being younger than everyone else in her grade, not noticeably pretty, not very popular, and a member of the high school debating team. She tends to stutter when she's nervous, which is frequently, and at times feels distanced from the two other members of her family. Her somewhat wimpish widower father lives elsewhere in town—worse still, he's an undertaker. (If Margie had been an MGM child her dad would have been a stolid, pipe-smoking attorney played by Walter Pidgeon; at Warner Brothers, a bluff telephone linesman played by an unhousebroken Alan Hale.) Margie's grandmother, whom she lives with, is an ex-suffragette who brooks no nonsense. ("I wish I was dead," says Margie, her whole world crumbling. "*Were* dead," says her grandmother.) The three men in Margie's life, in descending order of attractiveness and ascending order of availability, are Mr. Fontayne, Central High's hunky young French teacher ("my diary's simply *full* of him," Margie exclaims); Johnny "Jonnikins" Green, captain of the school football team; and Roy, a nerdish classmate who writes poetry in private but far from embodies it in public. The poetry section of the school library is where Margie lucks into her first moments alone with Mr. Fontayne, immediately after she has lost her bloomers to gravity for the first of three times in the story. Margie compounds her embarrassment by replying when asked if she like Keats: "I don't know, sir. What *are* Keats?"

Off to a good start, *Margie* keeps getting better and richer and funnier and more painful by the minute. In its next great scene the film re-creates a high school debate that is a treasure chest of inflated rhetoric, melodramatic gesticulation, and misplaced sarcasm. No sooner does Margie (one assumes) win her debate than we are whisked off to the town skating rink for perhaps the movie's finest sequence. Everyone on the ice—except of course Margie's escort Roy—is a good skater, particularly Margie's flapper friend and neighbor, Marybelle (a classic blonde cutie played by Barbara Lawrence, whose obvious skating expertise surely must have contributed to her subsequent cult status). Midway in the sequence the camera, stationed at center rink, executes a remarkable 540-degree pan as it follows skaters Margie and Jonnikins's graceful sliding waltz to the melody of "Three O'Clock in the Morning." The spell is broken when Margie loses her bloomers again (that's twice), but the day is saved by Mr. Fontayne who comes forward to discreetly shield the wayward garment from public scrutiny, then pocket it. Later that night he will call on Margie and return the bloomers. (This, by the way, is all more innocent than it sounds though perhaps less innocent than it was intended to be.)

The movie's last big sequence is the Senior Prom. Here, Margie, suddenly a swan, becomes the unexpected belle of

Jeanne Crain

the ball, and a touching subplot is resolved as shy father and neglected daughter discover how much they mean to each other. All ends with Margie losing her bloomers again (that's three times) and conveniently swooning.* Earlier in the scene, Vanessa Brown delivers the film's most deliciously satisfying line, which I won't spoil by divulging here, as Margie dances with Jonnikins while his date Marybelle fumes. Nor will I reveal whom Margie ultimately marries. The movie keeps this a secret until the very last scene, and it's a secret well worth saving for future *Margie* fans.

After all is said and done, *Margie* is a wonderful piece of Americana—a modest masterpiece whose relative lack of reputation remains a mystery. Its central role is played with charm and sensitivity by Jeanne Crain, a lovely Fox starlet who lacked the kind of charisma essential to major stardom; *Margie* was her one great moment. The picture was directed with considerable skill, affection, and humor by Henry King and was cooly photographed by Charles Clarke in the cold, clean, unsaturated colors of winter; one notable exception: a very brief, rosy-pink, single-shot scene in which we discover a happy Margie in her bubble bath, scrubbing herself and singing "April Showers" as her head and limbs are circled by a doting camera and by a totally unnaturalistic flock of large, floating soap bubbles—a *Margie* moment destined for a cherished place in America's collective memory. (This is one of many interludes in which *Margie* almost but not quite becomes a musical as cast or soundtrack breaks into "My Time Is Your Time," "Charmaine," "Avalon," "Diane," "Charles-

---

Margie's *New York Times* reviewer, "at the risk," he said, "of sounding prudish," called this great running gag "a running embarrassment."

ton," and other evocative vintage tunes.) Another magic moment for the memory bank captures a sadder Margie drifting off to sleep in her attic bedroom to the distant strains of "I'll See You in My Dreams."

There are two major categories of moviegoers who given the opportunity are likely to fall in love with Margie and *Margie*: 1. any American woman able to recall her adolescence with at least mixed if not positive emotions, and 2. anybody and everybody else.

★

THE BEST-
Cast American Movie

★

A southern military college is faced with a moral crisis when a malevolent cadet attempts to effect the dishonorable discharge of an innocent fellow student. The movie is *The Strange One*, a film that became an instant cult classic upon its release in 1957 (at my high school, anyway); that year, only *Sweet Smell of Success* rivaled it in sheer abundance of quotable dialogue and sinister epiphanies. Created by the brilliant writer Calder Willingham and directed modestly but with style by Jack Garfein, *The Strange One* is notable for its uncannily apt actor/character matchups:

Pat Hingle, Arthur Storch, George Peppard, and Ben Gazzara

Jocko de Paris . . . . BEN GAZZARA

Jocko is referred to variously as "a sadistic bully," "a card—the ace of spades," and "about the lowest darn creature I've ever seen in my life." When we first see him he's wearing a white service cap, black boxer shorts, black dress shoes and stockings, black garters, and a Hawaiian shirt. His entire wardrobe, in fact, proves more appropriate to a highborn New Orleans pimp than a boy in military school. Played by a young and handsome Ben Gazzara with sleek Mediterranean skill, Jocko is an insouciant Iago with the heavy-lidded face of a lizard, the low, uninflected voice of a male escort, and the blasé bearing and sly, mock-formal syntax of a nobleman about to strip and eat one of his peasants ("you freshmen seem shocked by our friendly visit—and disturbed by our continued presence here").

Robert Marquales . . . . GEORGE PEPPARD
Dead solid perfect as the cadet who finally blows the whistle on de Paris, Peppard seemed to have everything it takes to seduce American moviegoers, male and female alike, but somehow major stardom eluded him. I'll always remember him fondly for *The Strange One* and for the way he instinctively keeps trying to protect—even as he yearns to strangle—his hapless, hopeless roommate, Simmons.

Simmons . . . . ARTHUR STORCH
Simmons is an obnoxious, bucktoothed, unbathed nerd whose cowardice, piety, and spitefulness inspire in Jocko what raw meat does in lions. Arthur Storch's hilarious portrayal is so accomplished you end up almost feeling a little sorry for the twerp.

Harold Koble . . . . PAT HINGLE
Hingle was well into his thirties when he played Jocko's roommate, but he's nonetheless ideally cast as a good-time Charlie who'll go along with just about anything if there's a laugh in it. Not a bad sort at heart, he's basically nothing more than a big, naive, all-American boy, and that's why it takes him so long to catch on to Jocko's Old World game.

Rosebud . . . . JULIE WILSON
Julie Wilson's gaunt, sexy beauty was ideally suited to the

role of "Rosebud," the dim-witted morsel of town trash Jocko toys with. Much to Wilson's credit she made no attempt to "bring" anything to the character that wasn't there; having been trained as a singer rather than an actress, she probably had never read the entry for Southern women in *The Student Actor's Handbook*: "Play as insane." She would have been my first choice for Bonnie in *Bonnie and Clyde*.

Cadet Colonel Corger . . . . MARK RICHMAN
Corger is honorable, forceful, clearheaded, the kind of no-nonsense individual you would choose to lead you into battle or marry your airhead sister.

Roger Gatt . . . . JAMES OLSON
Gatt is big, strong, sullen, handsome, a prototype for the children's insult "If he had a brain he'd be dangerous."

Perrin McKee . . . . PAUL E. RICHARDS
A creepier version of Jerry Lewis, McKee is writing a paean to Jocko called *Night Boy*. A treat for the politically incorrect.

Major Avery . . . . LARRY GATES
Gates is a bit "actorish" compared with the younger players but quite affecting in his big confrontational scene with Jocko/Gazzara.

Georgie Avery . . . . GEOFFREY HORNE
Avery is a nice, clean-cut kid. No match for Jocko.

And so on down the line, straight through to the extras. In

addition to being Hollywood's most appropriately populated film, *The Strange One* has an even more remarkable distinction: Among movies cast essentially with New York-trained actors, it's one of the few that won't send you at some point screaming from the theater.

★

THE BEST
Avant-garde Short

★

Kenneth Anger's *Scorpio Rising* is an intoxicating stew of imagery and iconography, set to a sound track of thirteen pop records of the time (the early '60s), which are linked by the *vrooms* of motorcycle engines. The movie has no scenario to speak of, but if you insist: Various bikers groom themselves and their machines for a costume party which degenerates into an infantile homosexual orgy and then a quasi-Nazi rally; ultimately, one of them runs his cycle off the road and is killed. This "story" is told through an endless stream of masterfully montaged flotsam and jetsam: Nazi souvenir-shop kitsch, motorcycle paraphernalia, rough-trade motorcycle garb and gear, necrophilic symbols (including skulls and scorpions galore), clips from *The Wild One* and an old Jesus bio-pic, wax figures of Bela Lugosi as Dracula and of Gary Cooper as Marshal Will Kane, comic-strip panels, and even a shot of Mickey Rooney as a crowing Pan, an image that is inserted to rhyme with the Sunday-funnies Puck logo and epigraph ("What fools ye Mortals be") that begin the film. That the whole is so much greater than its paltry parts is due to Anger's astonishingly advanced sense of cinematic rhythm. So sound, indeed, is his cinepoetic pulse that the pop singles he appropriated to accompany his imagery have taken on new stature and even different meanings than they had possessed pre-Anger; before I first saw *Scorpio Rising*, Ricky Nelson's rockabilly version of "Fools Rush In" struck me as a catchy, pleasant, but essentially bland rendition of the Tin Pan Alley standard, but now, thanks to Kenneth Anger, I can't hear it without feeling a buzz of excitement and expectation. Some years after the movie was released, Anger, a notorious eccentric, accused George Lucas of ripping off *Scorpio Rising*'s pop-music sound-track conceit in Lucas's *American Graffiti*. That's a little like Ray Charles getting ticked off at David Clayton Thomas. *American Graffiti* is rock and roll as innocuous nostalgia; *Scorpio Rising* is rock and roll as narcotic and as nightmare.

★

THE BEST

Foreign Movie for People Who Don't Like Foreign Movies

★

High aloft an abandoned office building in a large office carpeted in sand and sparsely furnished with desks, a bed, a stove, and an airplane, lives a young survivor of the coming nuclear holocaust; his only comforts: an audiocassette player, a book, somebody's family photos, and a life-sized plastic doll. We first encounter our hero in conjugal embrace with his inflatable roommate, his pleasure rudely interrupted when his ardor causes her to rupture and deflate. Later, under siege by a gang of marauders, he shatters the windows of his hideaway, escapes in his open plane, flies out over the surrounding desert, and alights in a ghost city where he sets up housekeeping in what once was a barroom, feeding himself on booze and the fruits of an occasional fish storm. After being severely wounded by a scarred and bespectacled warrior-plunderer nearly twice his size, he staggers into the stronghold of a kindly doctor who nurses him back to health.

Following a few more run-ins with his giant nemesis our little pioneer encounters a female of his species.

Directed by twenty-three-year-old Luc Besson, *Le Dernier Combat* is a fascinating and marvelously elemental tale that splendidly captures the thrill of adventure, the excitement of discovery, the pain of loneliness, and—in the relationship between the doctor and the protagonist—the comfort and joy of fellowship.

Virtually the entire weight of the movie is shouldered by its imagery, a rich buffet of picturesque rubble, decayed architecture, and assorted small hardware, all dramatically, impeccably photographed in black-and-white Panavision—for, with the exception of one brief exchange, there is not a word of dialogue throughout. Far from being a pretentious conceit on Besson's part, this is an essential plot element: "Nuclear pollution has rendered the few survivors of the apocalypse totally mute. (The lone bit of dialogue: After taking a couple of healthy hits from an oxygen mask, the doctor and our hero haltingly exchange the word *"Bonjour."*) So if an aversion to subtitling and muckle-mouthed dubbing has kept you away from foreign films in the past, *Le Dernier Combat* may be just the import you've been waiting for. I can't promise you'll like Besson's prize-winning movie as much as I do, but if you know what *bonjour* means, I can guarantee you'll understand every word of it. (For the record: *Bonjour* is French for *howdy*.)

★

THE BEST
"Hitchcock Movie" Not Directed by Hitchcock

★

Back in 1933 when Alfred Hitchcock was still in England making rather genteel thrillers, Paramount released a parapsychological chiller that served up a fair portion of Hitchcock-like suspense while anticipating some of the slickness and gloss that Hitchcock's films were to accrue, for better or worse, when he hit Hollywood in 1939. Directed by Victor Halperin, who had sired *White Zombie* the year before, *Supernatural* is the story of a glamorous young heiress who is victimized by a fortune-hunting pseudo-spiritualist until the soul of a recently fried multimurderess enters the heroine's body to foil the scheme. The movie's Hitchcockian elements include a roving camera, plenty of elegant and cogent camera setups, an eschewal of surprise tactics in favor of suspense, and the presence of a coolly beautiful society blonde (Carole Lombard), a stiffly handsome, rather boneheaded leading man (Randolph Scott), an oily, faintly effeminate villain (Alan Dinehart), and a comic prole (Beryl Mercer). On the other hand, *Supernatural* is considerably more florid and melodramatic than the typical Hitchcock movie, and a whole lot creepier—right from its opening credits sequence, a witch's brew of thunder, lightning, louring clouds, and Wagnerian moaning. Among *Supernatural*'s most unsettling passages: a memorable Jekyll-into-Hyde moment by Lombard in which she signifies more with an arched eyebrow than many Hitchcock blondes did with their full bodies in entire films.

★

THE BEST
Happy Ending

★

The reason the ending of Preston Sturges's *Christmas in July* is the most intoxicating happy ending in movies is that *nobody knows it's a happy ending but we*, the audience.

For Jimmy MacDonald, a young white-collar drone who dreams about success and riches, it's been a decidedly up-and-down day. First he's informed he has won twenty-five thousand (1941) dollars in a slogan-writing contest, a turn of events that launches him on a major shopping spree, buying an engagement ring for his girl, and gifts for his mother and for everyone in his lower–middle-class neighborhood. Then comes the bad news: The whole thing was an office prank— he hasn't won the contest after all. All the gifts will have to be returned and with them all his hopes for a new life. Late that night Jimmy (Dick Powell) and his fiancée, Betty (Ellen

Drew), visit the new private office he's been awarded by his boss, impressed with Jimmy's windfall, along with a promotion and an increase in salary. A black cat rubs up against Jimmy's leg, and Betty asks Sam, the night porter, if black cats are a sign of good luck or bad. That all depends on what happens afterward, replies Sam. Jimmy's boss appears and, after being told that Jimmy, in fact, has not won the contest, revokes Jimmy's raise but allows him to keep his new title and private office on a trial basis. Jimmy and Betty glumly agree that this is something, at least, to be thankful for, and as they start to leave, the black cat rubs up against Jimmy for a second time. The disappointed couple are waiting for the elevator to take them down to the street and back into the rat race when *suddenly!* we are hurtled across town to the offices of the company that is sponsoring the contest. They have just picked a winner—and it's Jimmy MacDonald! We now return to an unsuspecting Jimmy and Betty stepping into the elevator as the most stirring phrases of the film's theme song, "Penthouse Serenade," rise on the sound track. The last thing we see is the charmed cat—lying across the bottom of the screen and looking straight at us—being lifted up and out of the frame, as if by a rising elevator but actually by a title card reading THE END.

★

THE BEST
Extended Sequence

★

When Andrew Sarris called Jean Renoir's *French Cancan* "the most joyous hymn to the glory of art in the history of cinema," he wasn't exaggerating. The lightest of masterpieces—by this I mean the least solemn, not the least substantial—and the most sumptuous, *French Cancan* offers in its final two reels a dazzling, almost overwhelming feast of color, motion, sound, and mass euphoria. A bit of exposition: After numerous complications, Danglard (Jean Gabin), the veteran impresario, has managed finally to open the doors of his new Montmartre nightclub, the Moulin Rouge, and all of *Belle-Epoque* Paris has turned out for the occasion. The high point of the evening is to be Danglard's revival of the cancan, featuring the talents of Nini (Françoise Arnoul), a pretty young laundress he has discovered and made his principal dancer. To complicate matters, each of Danglard's three latest mistresses will be appearing in the show: Lola (Maria Félix), who's fallen out of Danglard's favor; Nini, who's on her way out; and Esther, who's on her way in.

What follows is a sequence that once seen is never forgotten—it has *everything*: glorious, profligate color (to have seen *French Cancan* in a good 35mm print is to have been to Movie Heaven); suspense (after discovering Danglard with Esther,

Nini threatens to scuttle the show by refusing to perform); histrionics (Gabin gets to deliver one of his inimitable harangues, a show-must-go-on lecture directed at Nini); spice (Lola does a tasteful striptease as Catherine the Great); song (Esther sings the now familiar "La Complainte de la Butte" in the Edith Piaf manner*); plus tumbling bears, a drum corps of Russian grenadiers, and a whistling Pierrot clown. Last and best of all is the cancan itself, heralded by the emergence of dancing girls from seemingly everywhere: One drops over the edge of a balcony; others fly across tabletops and into and out of the laps of patrons; some materialize from backstage—one dancer literally bursts through a wall. A splendid commotion ensues as the girls fight their way through hordes of exuberant customers to converge on the dance floor and begin the show, while the Moulin Rouge's ecstatic clientele cheer them on, crowd them, and insinuate themselves into the dance itself. Renoir's cinematographer, Michel Kelber, shoots the cancan (still delightfully lewd after more than a century) from virtually every camera position, angle, and distance imaginable and the dancers' costumes (the girls are dressed in dark skirts and stockings, white petticoats and drawers, and blouses and bonnets of assorted hues) create an intoxicating kaleidoscope of whirling color. As the dancing and the tumult rise to higher and higher levels of excitement, we see, among the onlookers, various of the story's characters in new pairings—Lola with Danglard's financial backer, Nini's jilted boyfriend with her girlfriend from the laundry, Danglard with an auspicious young blonde he has spotted in the crowd—and just when everything is reach-

*Piaf herself performs in the film's previous sequence.

ing a fever pitch of happy frenzy, the sequence reverts to its initial shot, a long shot of the exterior of the Moulin Rouge. There we see a tiny, drunken figure in full evening dress (said to be Renoir) doff his top hat, take a deep bow, and stagger off the screen as the movie ends.

★

THE BEST
Credits Sequence

★

In 1955, graphic designer Saul Bass, aided immeasurably by composer Elmer Bernstein, ushered in the golden age of credits sequences with his bold design for the main titles of *The Man With the Golden Arm.* Seven years later Bass and Bernstein collaborated on an even more dynamic opening sequence, one which, unfortunately, few have seen, because it prefaced one of the most godawful movies of its time. It all begins innocently enough with a piquant percussive musical intro and the Columbia logo; then we find ourselves looking into the openings of a pile of ducts as the film's first credit appears, superimposed neatly across the mouth of a large duct and followed by the bright eyes of a black cat. The camera moves in; the cat's eyes look left, right, then straight at us; and *wham!*—Bernstein's score kicks in with its exciting, almost deafening signature theme as the name of the movie, WALK ON THE WILD SIDE, appears in white underneath the cat's eyes and across its screen-filling black face. Dissolve to an overhead tracking shot of the cat walking (momentarily through its own eyes) in slow motion as cast credits start to appear on the left. Dissolve to a left-to-right tracking shot of the prowling cat with Barbara Stanwyck's white credit super-imposed across virtually its entire length. Dissolve to a close-up of the cat's front paws, still pacing in slo-mo sync to the theme music. This series of lateral tracking shots continues as the cat literalizes the movie's title by walking behind and then through a slatted fence, in front of and then behind some chain-link fencing, behind and then between several photogenically cracked and rotting ducts—and finally stopping to size up a white cat that has crossed its path. (The black cat, by the way, was not a professional but a recruit from the Bass household.) Black cat attacks white cat and a fierce scrap ensues until the white cat turns tail and retreats and our hero(ine), little the worse for wear, resumes its journey. Ultimately, after the credits have informed us who produced and directed the turkey we're about to see, the story begins and the excitement ends.

★

THE BEST

Kissing Scene

★

Near the end of *Gregory's Girl*, a gentle comedy from Scotland, occurs my candidate for best all-time kissing scene, quantitatively as well as qualitatively speaking (I counted nine kisses—and the scene is picked up in the middle, at that). Gregory is a typically hopeless teenager, gawky and good-natured, who somehow has secured a date with the woman of his dreams, Dorothy, the most beautiful and athletic girl in school. Dorothy fails to show up, however, and instead dispatches a relay team of three classmates— Carol, Margo, and Susan—to stand in for her. Each girl in her turn escorts a confused Gregory around town until finally he realizes he's the victim of a female conspiracy to pair him off with Susan, who's sweet on him. ("It's just the way girls work," Susan explains. "They help each other.") All's well that ends well, nevertheless; at evening's end we find Gregory and Susan in the shadows of Gregory's front doorway where she is critiquing the latest of apparently several kisses he's just given her: "That's good. You've stopped kissing me like I was your auntie." The scene continues with boy and girl joking and giggling about this and that—they've already begun to develop their own private jokes—but never letting too long an interval elapse between kisses. Although he's a head taller than she, their kissing is not of the comically inept variety traditionally attributed to movie adolescents but is disarmingly straight, affectionate, sweet, and cumulatively sexy. Later in his bedroom Gregory's ten-year-old sister and romantic advisor, Madeline, cross-examines him: "Did you kiss her?" "No," he replies, "maybe tomorrow." "You liar," she says, "I saw you! You kissed her about fifty times!" After a bit more postdate evaluation Madeline wonders, "Who's going to be Gregory's girl?" "You are," he says and turns in for the night to dream presumably about Susan. Somewhere outside in the dark, meanwhile, having done her good deed for the day, Dorothy takes her nightly jog.

★

THE BEST
Medium Close-up

★

A medium close-up is a camera shot that confines itself to its subject's head and shoulders. Late in *The Public Enemy* occurs a medium close-up that is head and shoulders above most other shots of its kind. James Cagney's boyhood pal and crime partner has just been killed by a rival gang. As nearly a dozen members of that gang file in to a storefront for a post-hit huddle, Cagney watches from across the street, protected from the pelting rain by only his black, tilted, felt hat and the turned-up collar of his black suit jacket. Cut to the shot under discussion (hold on to your hearts): Cagney, his face glistening with rain, half-smiles malevolently; his beautiful, wide-set eyes narrow in anticipation; and then his lips part and pull back upon themselves and seem to disappear behind his teeth in a ghoulish grin of pure evil. This shot must have scared the hell out of 1931 moviegoers, who were not to be introduced to Cagney's more amiable side until a bit later in his career. The image is held for only a few seconds, then Cagney, hands jammed in pockets, stalks toward the camera and into the storefront. We hear gunfire and screams. Cagney staggers out, guns in hand, then hurls them through the storefront window. Severely wounded, he lurches and coughs his way along a Brobdingnagian curbstone and, just before collapsing in a puddle, announces to the world "I ain't so tough"—but any soul brave enough to still be watching knows better.

★

THE BEST

Mad Scene

★

"**N**uns are clearly box-office, aren't they?" observed Michael Powell in his autobiography, *A Life in Movies*. "Well, I was sleeping with one of those nuns and will always be in love with another. I reckoned that I could make one of the most subtly erotic films ever made." Powell was talking about *Black Narcissus*—if not one of the most erotic films ever made, certainly one of the most dazzling.

An order of Anglican nuns has established a convent high in the windswept Himalayas where they fall victim to a variety of unfamiliar longings and neurasthenic disorders induced by the exotic locale, culture, and climate ("there's something in the atmosphere that makes everything seem exaggerated"). Especially afflicted is Sister Ruth, a high-strung young woman whose jealousy toward Sister Clodagh (the Sister Superior) combined with sexual hysteria has driven her to the brink of madness. Sister Clodagh is played by Deborah Kerr; Sister Ruth, by Kathleen Byron, a slender and strikingly photogenic actress endowed with the sharp nose, chin, and cheekbones of a Celtic sorceress. Her mad scene—mad sequence, actually—begins with Sister Clodagh, in the midst of her nightly rounds, startled to discover a bareheaded Sister Ruth wearing makeup and a red civilian dress. Sister Ruth spitefully de-

clares that she has renounced her vows and is leaving the
order at once. After Sister Clodagh exhorts her to stay, at
least until morning, the two women, locked in a battle of
wills, seat themselves at a table to wait out the night. Sister
Clodagh immerses herself in her prayer book; across the table
Sister Ruth reapplies her lip rouge; eventually Sister Clodagh
falls asleep and Sister Ruth flees the convent, descends to the
valley, and fights her way through a small jungle to arrive at
the house of Mr. Dean (David Farrar), a rudely attractive
young Englishman with whom she has become infatuated.
Sweat gleaming through the powder on her flushed face, she
declares her love to Dean; he rebuffs her and offers to
accompany her back to the convent. Convinced (not entirely
without justification) that Dean and Sister Clodagh are in
love, Sister Ruth returns to the convent in a venomous,
paranoid rage.

It is now early morning. A despondent Sister Clodagh is on
her way to chapel when a shock cut assaults us with an
extreme close-up of Sister Ruth's crazed eyes and fevered
brow beneath red ringlets drenched with perspiration. In
chapel Sister Clodagh senses someone spying on her and we
are given a split-second glimpse of the mad Sister Ruth
scuttling up a flight of stairs like a spider. We see Sister
Clodagh wearily making her way up the path outside the
convent walls; meanwhile Sister Ruth, as daft as a drifting
feather, scampers along the dark interior walls. As Sister
Clodagh begins tolling the convent bells at the edge of a
precipitous cliff, the door to the convent is swept open by
Sister Ruth who appears to us in one of the cinema's most
bloodcurdlingly beautiful shots. As bony as death, as gray and

David Farrar, Deborah Kerr, and Kathleen Byron

clammy as the stormy sea, she pauses in the doorway, emerges, and—murder in her black-rimmed eyes—slowly walks toward us and toward Sister Clodagh who is still tolling matins only inches away from an 8,000-foot drop . . .

Powell created these last few minutes of high melodrama through an unusual technique: Reversing the customary procedure, he had the sequence's music sound track composed prior to shooting, then staged and shot the sequence to conform with the track's preordained rhythms. Powell, who was justifiably proud of the sequence, reflected: "I had become accustomed to regarding music as something you brought to the film to increase its theatrical effect, after the actual shooting was finished. It can only have been a kind of restless ambition and subconscious desire to experiment, which made me want to reverse the order of things . . . It worked! I have never enjoyed myself so much in my life . . . I was so happy! I swore that this was the only way to make films . . . In *Black Narcissus*, I started out almost as a documentary director and ended up as a producer of opera."

★

THE BEST
Musical Showstopper

★

"**H**ow Could You Believe Me When I Said I Love You When You Know I've Been a Liar All My Life" is Hollywood's longest song title and one of its best numbers. It's also the definitive showstopper—that is, it has nothing to do with the plot of the movie at hand (in this case MGM's *Royal Wedding*), it was deliberately created to knock audiences off their seats, and it is followed by ample screen time for inevitable applause. A grab bag of song, dance, patter, and shtick patterned on classic vaudeville and burlesque routines and performed by Fred Astaire and Jane Powell, "HCYBMWISILYWYKIBALAML" takes the form of a lovers' quarrel between two low-rent types—she bemoaning his insincerity and infidelity; he essentially and unrepentantly owning up to everything. Fred is decked out in mustard shirt and socks, teeny-weeny bow tie, straw boater (soon to be destroyed by a peeved Powell), black-and-white shoes, and a checkered jacket buttoned about a foot below the sternum-high waistband of his French blue trousers. Jane's a shade less garish in umber and gold topped with orange-pink beret and auburn curls. The number begins with some nifty patter:

> **HIM:** All right, so I said it, so you hoid it, so you mean it—so what!
>
> **HER:** So you're always makin' cracks, makin' cracks.
>
> **HIM:** Like what?
>
> **HER:** Like always *hyoom*alatin' me, *hyoom*alatin' me. Dincha mother never teach you no manners?
>
> **HIM:** I never had no mudder. We was too poor.

The song itself is the craftiest of crowd-pleasers, a delightful duet of mutual dissatisfaction that is less a cat-and-mouse game than a cat-and-dog fight. One of its most appealing qualities is the manner in which it unexpectedly switches back and forth between a torchy, wha-wha theme and a jumpy, double-time (EX-er-ci-ses, EX-er-ci-ses) motive. The dancing is an old-fashioned delight. Abrupt leaps occur out of nowhere and several melodramatic poses are struck and frozen. Astaire's hopped-up, loose-as-a-goose performance represents his most successful excursion into the lower social depths—and also his broadest (at one point he literally laughs up his sleeve at Jane's pleas); Powell holds up her end of things surprisingly well (MGM singers could dance better than most dancers); and both of them prove it *is* possible to hoof and chew gum at the same time. This is how it all ends. Jane beats Fred up and finishes him off with a venerable bit of burlesque business: She steadies him, places his fist under his chin and his knee under his elbow, then winds up and boots the bottom of his foot, setting off a chain reaction that leaves a floored Fred, hat around neck, doing a backstroke to escape further battering. Meanwhile a hovering, finger-jabbing Powell pursues his retreating body offstage. Even the curtain call is in character, with both combatants stone-facing each other and the audience, and Jane, still playing Maggie to Fred's Jiggs, figuratively leading him around by a leash as MGM's off-camera audience joins generation after generation of moviegoers in ecstatic applause.

★

THE BEST
Opening Sequence in a Western

★

Arickety door of slatted wood squeals open. A toothless old man in a railway cap apprehensively turns and sees a huge pair of boots, followed—as the camera travels upward—by an ankle-length duster, a shotgun, a gun belt, and, finally, the large, stolid face of Woody Strode who is gazing at him from beneath the mammoth brim of a black hat. The old man turns again to see, framed in other doorways, two more men, each wearing the same kind of black hat and long coat as Strode. Everything is motionless but the wind-blown dusters. Surrounded, the old man haltingly begins to advise his visitors, one of whom is Jack Elam, that train tickets are to be purchased only outside, but Elam's walleyed stare persuades him to make an exception. The third member of the armed trio amuses himself by chattering, like a demented monkey, at a caged bird as the old stationmaster hands Elam three tickets and requests payment. Elam allows the tickets to slip through his fingers, smiles unsympathetically, seizes the old man by the neck, shunts him into an alcove, and slams a door shut on him with a deafening roar—in the process blacking out the screen. A white credit line tells us we are about to see

A SERGIO LEONE FILM. The credits continue as a native woman, who has been loitering about, hastily escapes into the dusty distance of an endless landscape. We are clearly in the middle of nowhere. The three men, who seem to be waiting for somebody or something, begin to occupy themselves in their separate ways: Strode tends to his horse, Elam settles into a chair, and the third man sits outside and cracks his knuckles. The telegraph machine comes to life and Elam silences it with a tug of his hand. Condensation from a water tower starts to drip on Woody Strode's shaven head, which he shelters by putting on his hat. The rhythmic *thwumps* made by the water dripping onto his hat seem to please him. Something keeps squeaking. A fly arrives to annoy Elam and we watch it explore, in Panavision close-up, his lightly bearded face. His repeated attempts to shoo the fly with his breath and his face muscles are unsuccessful; the fly is here to stay. At long last the fly alights on the wall, where Elam, with a very quick movement, traps it in the barrel of his gun. Carefully, he stops up the gun barrel with his finger and, cradling the gun to his cheek, contentedly listens to the augmented buzzing of the trapped fly. A train approaches. Strode, in enormous close-up, lifts his hat to his lips and, with great seriousness and deliberation, drinks the water that has collected in the brim. As the train pulls into the station Elam liberates the fly, Strode loads his shotgun, and all three men, at some distance from each other, approach the train, which eventually screeches to a halt. We are now ten minutes into the movie.

Whomever it is that these men have come to meet appears not to have arrived. As the train starts to pull out of the station, they turn and are about to leave the scene when they are stopped short by the plaintive sound of a harmonica. Playing the instrument is Charles Bronson, who apparently has exited the train from the far side. Bronson stops playing and we hear the ominous first notes of the movie's score (composed, the credits have told us, by Ennio Morricone). After a certain amount of ensemble glaring Bronson asks Elam about someone named Frank. "Frank sent *us*," Elam replies. "Did you bring a horse for me?" asks Bronson. Elam (spell it backwards) looks around and sees only three horses. "Looks like we're shy one horse," he says with mean amusement. His cohorts laugh. Bronson, with an almost imperceptible shake of his head, says, "You brought two too many"—and the screen erupts from all sides with the massive timpani of gunfire. Approximately two-and-a-half hours later we will be informed that the name of the movie we've been watching is *Once Upon a Time in the West*.

★

THE BEST
Neil Simon Adaptation

★

The Sunshine Boys is the tragicomic story of a vaudeville comedy team who reunite, after many years apart, in order to recreate one of their classic routines for a television special, but it's the reluctant reunion of two men totally incompatible in temperament. In fact the only thing Al Lewis and Willy Clark have in common, other than an interest in trade gossip, is encroaching senility. Each man has the same maddening habit of bouncing back an acquired piece of information as though it were his own idea; for example, when Willie's nephew Ben remarks of the door to Willy's apartment that Willy will "probably have to oil it," Willy replies, "I think I have to oil it." Al Lewis is similarly afflicted. Consider the early part of the conversation that ensues when Ben pays Al a visit:

BEN: It was nice of you to see me.

AL: Really? When was that?

BEN: Today. *Laughs nervously.* It was nice of you to see me today.

AL: Certainly. Today is fine. As a matter of fact I was expecting you today.

Willy Clark is a man whose mental untidiness extends to his rooms, his wardrobe, his family relationships, his whole life. Rendered virtually unemployable by his age and his skill at alienating if not infuriating anyone in a position to hire him, Willy is a self-destructive paranoiac, or, in the more apposite words of his ex-partner, "a seventy-three-year-old putz." Al Lewis, in contrast, is a reasonable and placid soul who has retired to New Jersey where he lives contentedly with his daughter and grandchildren. The duo's reunion engagement ends, predictably, in a shambles when Willie's propensity for paranoid hysteria triggers a heart attack, and the movie concludes at Willie's sickbed with Lewis and Clark continuing a series of debates about whether it was Saul Burton or Sid Bernstein who was the manager of the Belasco Theatre, whether he was the manager of the Belasco or the Morosco Theatre, whether it was Bernie Eisenstein or Jackie Aaronson who was Rodriguez of Ramona and Rodriguez (or was it Lopez of DeMarco and Lopez?), and so on, and so on, and so forth. As the two old troupers continue their reminiscences seemingly into infinity, we realize that much as they antagonize each other, each is all the other now has left. A shared past and the idleness of old age has united them at last—if not in affection, than in companionship—as Neil Simon's very very funny, very very sad story ends.

George Burns and Walter Matthau are brilliant as Lewis and Clark (though not, oddly enough, in the one vaudeville routine we see them perform), but with all due respect to Mr. Burns's immaculate performance, the Best Supporting Actor Oscar he won for *The Sunshine Boys* really should have gone to Richard Benjamin for his enormously affecting portrayal of Willy Clark's long-suffering nephew/agent/guardian angel Ben. When that performance, one of the best small jobs of acting I've ever seen, went unnominated, any lingering faith I had in the validity of the Academy Awards vanished forever.

Postscript: Sitting near me at a Florida bar, a group of aspiring junior-executive types, uniformly dressed in business suits, white shirts, and bland ties, tire of discussing the Dolphins' prospects and break into a series of familiar one-liners: "The finger! You're starting with the finger again!"; "As an actor no one could touch him. As a human being no one wanted to touch him"; "Yes—with an *against it*!"; "Entaaah!" I realize, somewhat to my pleasant surprise, that these fair-haired boys are trading, with the enthusiasm of aficionados, pet lines from *The Sunshine Boys*. A strange thought occurs to me: If a movie about a pair of seedy New York–Jewish ex-vaudevillians can achieve cult status among young, upwardly mobile, southern WASPs, what, I wonder, is next: midnight screenings of *Metropolitan* at the Apollo Theatre?

★

THE BEST
Science-Fiction Movie

★

My list of favorite science-fiction movies would make most sci-fi fans snicker, but as the average sci-fi freak strikes me as an over-IQ'd adolescent who never grew up, this doesn't bother me. The kind of soft-core science-fiction I favor is best exemplified by *The Man Who Could Work Miracles*, a comedy of ideas that is totally unburdened with bug-eyed monsters, cuddly aliens, interplanetary odysseys, space wars, time travel, stultifying utopias, and high-tech gadgetry. What's more, the whole thing is set in a quiet English town in the mid-1930s (when the movie was made)—a time and a place as remote from the futuristic Armageddons of current sci-fi fare as a blush is from a rash. Most fantasy classics—*The Thief of Baghdad*, for instance—are essentially children's films with a generous portion of adult diversions, but *The Man Who Could Work Miracles* is the exact opposite: a grown-up movie that kids too will love. An expansion of and an improvement on the H. G. Wells story of the same name, it begins quite splendidly with three gods. (George Sanders, in his first year in films, plays the god Indifference, a startlingly prophetic role considering his subsequent typecasting.) One of them, much against the advice of his colleagues, decides to bestow absolute power on a random earthling. The winner of this

Sophie Stewart, Roland Young, and Gertrude Musgrove

celestial sweepstakes turns out to be a department store floorwalker named George McWhirter Fotheringay (Roland Young). After working his first miracle in a local pub and being ejected by its literal-minded proprietor, Fotheringay, alone in his room, tests his new powers by conjuring up rabbits, goldfish, assorted fruit, and a kitten (which scratches him).

Most of the rest of the movie is devoted to Fotheringay's confused attempts to determine how best to use his omnipotence—a decision everyone who has ever known and/or ignored him wants to influence. His coworkers urge him to make himself rich; his employer wants Fotheringay to make him (the employer) richer; and a liberal clergyman exhorts him to use his cosmic clout to found a new age of global peace and plenty. Meanwhile Fotheringay, who has long loved one girl and lusted for another, discovers that his new capabilities don't extend to seduction. They do, however, encompass sedition; at one point he banishes a bothersome bobby first to Hell and then to San Francisco (the city in which anyone who has ever disappeared is said to have been seen, according to an Oscar Wilde character). Eventually a crusty old Tory colonel, offended by Fotheringay's class origins and his potential for begetting radical change, attempts to assassinate him— and that's when the worm finally turns. Here the film transforms itself from light fantasy into dark fable and we are presented with a spectacular climactic set piece that incorporates dizzying special effects, lavish costuming, a massive set, and a bravura stretch of declamatory acting by Roland Young, who was probably working off frustrations accumulated throughout years of playing repressed, prematurely middle-aged wimps like Fotheringay. (The new Young didn't take; a year later he would be cast as Topper.)

H. G. Wells (screenplay), Lothar Mendes (director), Alexander Korda (producer), Vincent Korda (sets), Michael Spolianski (score), Hal Rosson (photography), Ned Mann (special effects)—today these names serve to remind us of a fabulous age long, long ago when there were indeed men who could work miracles, and some of these men made movies.

★

THE BEST

Unhappy Ending

★

It is autumn in Vienna. Harry Lime, *The Third Man*, has just been buried. Among his mourners are Anna Schmidt, a young actress who loved him—even after learning he was an all-around wrongo—and Holly Martins, a decent but dull fellow who had been Harry's best friend, had reluctantly betrayed him, and has fallen in love with Anna. After the ceremony Holly, hoping against hope, stations himself at the side of the long, tree-lined thoroughfare upon which Anna is walking home. In a typical Hollywood movie she would walk straight into his arms. In an "honest" drama she would fly into hysterics and chew him out for having contributed to Harry's comeuppance and being a hopeless wimp to boot. But in *The Third Man* she does neither. In fact she does nothing, just walks and walks and walks and walks and walks—toward the camera, and, looking neither left nor right and without quickening her pace, right past Holly until she disappears into the off-camera foreground. The victim of the most thorough rejection the screen has ever displayed, Holly reaches into a pocket, pulls out a pack of cigarettes, and lights one up. Meanwhile, in the words of critic Vernon Young, "all the leaves in Vienna, it seems, fall from the sad and stately trees."

★

THE BEST

Adaptation of a Trashy Novel

★

In the late 1940s Mickey Spillane wrote a series of best-selling private-eye novels featuring Mike Hammer, a misogynistic brute whose violence-prone personality and sexual primitivism endeared him to millions of mass-market paperback readers, among them Ayn Rand. (At some point Rand and Spillane formed a mutual admiration society and for a while he served as House Lout of the political right's literary-cultural wing.) When it was announced that Robert Aldrich would direct Spillane's *Kiss Me Deadly*, it seemed an odd matchup—Aldrich having served his cinematic apprenticeship under such left-leaning luminaries as Jean Renoir, Charles Chaplin, Lewis Milestone, Joseph Losey, Robert Rossen, and

Jack Lambert, Ralph Meeker, and Jack Elam

Abraham Polonsky. Aldrich, indeed, disliked the novel and decided to subvert it by turning Mike Hammer into "a bedroom dick," a sleazy private investigator who specializes in divorce cases. This strategy backfired a bit when Ralph Meeker was cast as Hammer. Meeker, a good-looking, unpretentious Everymug, could play insensitive and even cruel but not sleazy, and as nearly everyone else in *Kiss Me Deadly* looks and acts as if he/she has a sublet in the sewers (with Gaby Rodgers, Paul Stewart, and Wesley Addy the standouts in an incomparably creepy cast), Meeker becomes our hero by default. Aldrich's true act of subversion was to unleash the most formally exciting and thematically resonant film to emerge from Hollywood since *Citizen Kane* fourteen years earlier. (It's a sad paradox that Aldrich's movie, which was ahead of its time, is even further ahead of ours.) Nearly every shot is interesting and/or unsettling; disorienting compositions and decapitating camera angles abound. Even the opening crawl is perverse; the credits, rather than moving from the bottom of the screen to the top, as is customary, proceed in reverse, so that at moments we find ourselves reading, for example:

DEADLY"   and   NAT "KING" COLE
"KISS ME   sung by
                            "RATHER HAVE THE BLUES"

What the hell is going on here anyway?

Something, it appears, about the pursuit of a box containing a radium fireball—a priceless but deadly package that is called "The Great Whatsit" by one character and turns out to be the McGuffin to end all McGuffins. Meanwhile, on the way to the apocalypse, Aldrich treats us to one of the most unnerving running displays of off-center sadism in screen history. A milestone in movie horror is reached in the first reel with a low shot of a woman's naked legs hanging over the side of a bed as her off-camera screams inform us she is being tortured—a particularly excruciating moment because at that point we have no idea what is going on or why. Later Mike Hammer terrorizes an aging opera singer simply by cracking one of the singer's rare Caruso 78s, and still later disciplines a venal morgue director by slamming a desk drawer on the old man's fingers and smiling at the shrieks that ensue. Finally, there is the Pandora's Box scene—visually, aurally, and dramatically the absolute ultimate in sheer "go-for-it" audacity;

it is an extraordinary scene that terminates an extraordinary movie and with it, perhaps, Mike Hammer. I say *perhaps* because there are two versions of *Kiss Me Deadly* in circulation. In the rarer and weaker version Hammer and his secretary (or "secretary"), Velda, survive the picture's climactic atomic holocaust by throwing themselves into the sea. In the other version they are presumably destroyed (although we don't actually see them die, we never see them escape). That one's the ending for me. I'd like to think that Aldrich so disliked Mike Hammer that the director chose to undermine one of the most sacred traditions of genre filmmaking by killing off his serial hero in the latter's prime (would that Dr. No had done the same to James Bond back in 1963). Whichever way you look at it, Robert Aldrich had brought the film noir era to an end not with a whimper but a Big Bang.

★

THE BEST
Dance Short

★

A tie between *Pas de Deux* and *Nine Variations on a Dance Theme*, two late '60s films that play with time and space in different but equally ingenious ways.

Norman McLaren's *Pas de Deux* is based on a uniquely

seductive optical technique by means of which a piece of
filmed movement is superimposed on itself at uniformly
staggered intervals. The nearest natural equivalent I can
think of is a stream of soap bubbles being blown through a
small wire hoop; on film, a primitive application of the process
can be seen in a 1950 William Bendix programmer, *Kill the
Umpire*, when baseball umpire Bendix, dazed by a beanball,
perceives the next pitch as a whole series of pitches delivered
in rapid succession. *Pas de Deux* bathes its dancers, Margaret
Mercier and Vincent Warren of Les Franda Ballets Canadiens,
in white light that silhouettes the outlines of their bodies
against and within an environment of pure black in a way that
makes them look neon enclosed, a pleasing semiabstract
effect in itself. At first the presiding optical conceit is used
rudimentarily: A Mercier movement is frozen at one side of
the frame and her "ghost" leaves her body to dance to the
other side of the frame, where it in turn freezes as the first
frozen image fades away. Then things become more complex:
the first image, instead of fading, follows its ghost, enters it,
and becomes one with it . . . the two images, both of them in
motion at the same time, perform the same movement, but
one has been given a head start on the other . . . the two
images perform the same movement side by side and unstag-
gered, but one of them is "flopped" and when it overlaps
with its twin a kaleidoscopic effect is created. When Warren
enters the frame to join Mercier, McLaren pulls out all the
optical stops in an awesome display of imagery that combines
the abstract and the human to spectacular effect. At times the
multiple superimpositions are so tightly staggered that the
white-lit dancers are transformed into liquefied blurs; less

closely staggered passages look like 3-D kaleidoscopes (when Mercier circles a stationary Warren, a lovely Maypole pattern is created); and particularly beautiful effects arise when—but why try to describe the indescribable? Fourteen minutes of white magic, *Pas de Deux* has to be seen to be believed.

Hilary Harris's *Nine Variations on a Dance Theme* is a bit more intellectual than *Pas de Deux* but only ostensibly less sensuous. A dancer, Bettie de Jong, dressed in full-length woolies, is alone in a bare, sunlit loft. She performs a fifty-second dance, which ends as it began, dancer prone, with right cheek and left palm to floor. The dance, which is performed counter-clockwise, is captured in a single clockwise shot. Then the dance is repeated, this time covered in a different traveling camera pattern. In the third variation edits start to appear, and in the fifth variation they start to overlap: A shot will begin at an earlier stage of the dance than the one which ended the previous shot (there are no dissolves in the film). By the time the final variation has concluded in a breathtaking series of time-overlapped dying falls, the gyroscopic photography and mix-and-match editing scheme have combined to cover the dancer and her dance, which itself is never varied, from a seemingly infinite variety of perspectives. As with *Pas de Deux*, the viewer is left with an impression not of abstract beauty but of superhuman beauty.

★

THE BEST

Comic Sermon

★

The Seduction of Mimi was a somewhat depressing and at moments tasteless Italian social comedy about a Sicilian laborer who becomes involved in the workers' movement but eventually is tamed by the established church/state/crime cartel in combination with his own deficiencies of character. Along the way, he leaves his wife for a more progressive woman, but his reactionary roots surface when he learns his wife has been impregnated by another man, at which point he totally loses his revolutionary cool and concocts an outrageous revenge scheme. A few years later the story was turned into *Which Way Is Up?*, a vehicle for Richard Pryor. If, perhaps, the property lost a couple of satiric teeth in its passage from southern Italy to southern California, the difference was more than made up in laughs. Pryor, one of our most underrated actors, plays three roles: the protagonist, the perennial victim—like his screen prototype Bob Hope—of his intrinsic cowardice and carnality; his father, a hilariously mean and dirty-mouthed old man; and, best of all, the Reverend Lenox Thomas, pastor of the 7-11 Lucky Church of Eternal Salvation. One of Pryor's most inspired characterizations, the Reverend Mr. Thomas is a master of evangelistic bombast and demi-operatic oratory—a shout-pause-shout specialist who is

incapable of getting through an entire sentence without un-
naturally elongating at least one word ("You're sick—at
heart—and your *miiiind*—is troubled"). We first meet Thomas
in his pulpit performing an upbeat hymn on electric guitar
accompanied by a female gospel choir and his wife, Sarah, on
piano, following which he proceeds to deliver a unique sermon to a rapt congregation:

"High *blood* presh-uhhh! Tooth decay! You get *all* these
things—when you sin and *lust*! I ain't got a cavity in my
mouth!" testifies the righteous reverend. "I must admit Sister
Sarah had *one* cavity . . . but I cleansed her of her sin and her
cavity filled itself!". At this point the speaker takes the heat
off one member of his family and transfers it to another. "You
know—I recall when my youngest, Junior here, Alfred, was
young . . . he used to *peee* on his brothers and sisters in
behhhd—when he was *yuuung*. And he came to me and said,
'Daddy, is that *siiin*?' I said, 'No! You have not *sinned*—unless
you do it on *pur*pose!' " Shouts of assent from the congregation, then the reverend comes to the crux of his lesson. "Now,
his sister *sinned*, because she used to pee back on him!!" And
here—after Pastor Thomas has paused to check out some of
the younger female members of his flock and deliver himself
of a few final words of uplift—endeth the sermon.

★

THE BEST
Trilogy

★

And the winner is . . . the *Porky's* trilogy.

Just kidding. In 1931 and 1932 Marcel Pagnol, France's most popular young playwright, brought his hit play *Marius* and its sequel, *Fanny*, to the screen; and in 1936 Pagnol personally directed *César*, which completed the story nearly a generation after its outset. This cycle of films, which came to be known as the *Fanny* trilogy (and sometimes the Marseilles trilogy), tells the story of Fanny, a girl who sells cockles in the street; Marius, the restless boy she loves; and Marius's father, César, a waterfront bar proprietor. This trio of characters is played by Orane Demazis, who gives a charming and animated performance as Fanny; Pierre Fresnay, whose broad and brilliantly high-strung portrayal of Marius contrasts sharply with his most famous role, the coolly aristocratic Boïeldieu in *Grand Illusion*; and Raimu as César in a performance of marvelous subtlety, humor and depth. Raimu was one of the major early exemplars of naturalistic sound-film acting (Orson Welles called him "the greatest actor in the world"); even when he appears to be overacting it's not Raimu who's hamming it up but César. Indeed, for many the most fondly remembered scenes from this six-and-a-half-hour saga are not the Fanny-Marius contretemps but the comic inter-

ludes of César and his cronies engrossed in gossip, cards, or
mutual needling.

We are not far here from formula fiction; the trilogy's plot
is so close to cliché, its component parts could have been
subtitled "The Call of the Wild," "Do the Right Thing,"
and "All's Well that Ends Well," respectively. If the themes
of the *Fanny* trilogy seem equally familiar it's because they
are major ones: the conflicts between freedom and responsi-
bility, parent and child, male and female, community sanc-
tions and individual longings—themes that have become
discredited only by the subversive uses to which they've been
put by the movie, TV, publishing, and advertising industries.

A measure of the singer-not-the-song inviolability of the
trilogy's spirit is its inevitable loss in translation: The "vehicle" was remade in Italy, in Germany, in 1938 by MGM (*Port
of Seven Seas*), on Broadway in 1954 (*Fanny*), and again by
Hollywood in 1960 (*Fanny*), but Pagnol's understanding of and
affection for his characters, their class, and their milieu were
dissipated by time, distance, and insincerity. Furthermore,
the idea of a *Fanny* without Raimu is inconceivable to anyone
who has seen the original. To many of us who have, it remains
one of the meaningful experiences of our moviegoing lives, a
priceless opportunity to enter the world of an immeasurably
valuable (and endlessly garrulous) community of good folk—
there are no villains in this tale—and linger there a precious
while as unseen guests. The story of a family in crisis, the
Fanny trilogy is "Masterpiece Theatre" transformed by love,
insight, wit, and commitment; if this be treacle, Pagnol made
the most of it.

In his time Pagnol was widely attacked by film theoreticians

Alida Rouffe and Raimu

as cinematically backwards—a wound he exacerbated with such rash public statements as: "The talking film is the art of printing, fixing, and propagating theater"—and to this day he is criticized for his alleged cinematic (not to mention social) conservatism, but it's a phony issue, I think; if Pagnol's films are uncinematic (whatever that means), let us not reject Pagnol but instead expand our definition of cinema. And while Pagnol continues to be belittled or ignored in intellectual, aesthetic, and politicized circles, he is in the process of being (re)discovered—eighteen years after his death—by popular audiences (his true following) via adaptations of *My Father's Glory* and *My Mother's Castle,* Pagnol's memoirs of his childhood, and of *Manon of the Spring.*

I urge any of you who have not yet seen the *Fanny* trilogy to do so, starting with the self-contained *Marius* and moving on, if you're so inclined, to *Fanny, César,* and the later Pagnol films: *Angele, Jofroi, Le Shpountz, The Baker's Wife, The Well-Digger's Daughter,* etc. It's a superbly personal body of work and a most seductive one.

Art's bottom line, for me, is not *what* is being communicated (content) or even *how* it's being communicated (form) but *who* is communicating it (sensibility). Marcel Pagnol had nothing earthshaking to say and he invented no radical ways of saying it, but there was only one Pagnol—he was an artist with a unique soul and that's why he's so valuable. To put it another way: Art isn't important, only artists are.

★

THE BEST

B Movie

★

A word about B movies: Chances are, your favorite B movie isn't really a B movie, strictly speaking, but a glum or depleted A movie. Ephraim Katz's film encyclopedia describes a *B picture* as "a low-budget film, usually shown on the lower half of a double feature program . . . While A pictures . . . were exhibited on the basis of a percentage of the box-office take, B pictures were rented for a fixed flat rate, regardless of attendance." According to this definition such classic sleepers as *The Asphalt Jungle, Nightmare Alley,* and *Out of the Past* aren't B pictures at all but low-key, low-budget A pictures; perhaps we should call them A minuses.

The Seventh Victim is an authentic B picture but not a typical one. Few B moviemakers, for starters, had either the time or the ambition to open a film with an epigraph, and certainly not one as morbid as this extract from the sonnets of John Donne: "I runne to death, and death meets me as fast, and all my pleasures are like yesterday." The story begins with a lengthy shot of a stately three-sectored stained-glass window abutting the staircase of a girls' private school—a solemn note that is sustained throughout the movie's seventy-one minutes as we accompany schoolgirl Mary Gibson (very affectingly played by Kim Hunter) in a search for her missing older sister

Jacqueline (Jean Brooks). Nothing along the way is allowed to detract from the picture's somberness of mood or seriousness of purpose, least of all comic relief. A Runyonesque private investigator, portrayed against type as a mild, rather meek little man, is allowed his measure of dignity as is, in fact, everyone in the movie—all the way down to the villains and bit players like the old Apple Annie–type newspaper hawker who startles us with her sober grace. Eschewing comedy, *The Seventh Victim does* permit itself a love interest of sorts, but only with hindsight do we realize that it may not be a hopeless love.

Halfway through the film Jacqueline makes her first appearance, hypnotizing us with her strange, pale beauty and raising the movie to a higher plane. It seems that Jacqueline has been in hiding from a band of Satanists who are pressuring her to kill herself as punishment for abandoning her membership in their sect. A death-obsessed neurotic by nature, Jacqueline has been reduced by her flirtation with Satanism to a state of severe melancholy; capable of only fitful resistance to the fate that awaits her, Jacqueline, in a way, has already begun to die.

The story concludes with a series of memorable scenes:

1. Mary is surprised in her shower by a cult member who speaks to her in silhouette through the curtain—a striking scene that anticipates *Psycho*'s shower sequence but is keyed to menace rather than mayhem.

2. The Satanists place a glass of poisoned wine before Jacqueline and for hours exhort her to drink.

3. A man with a knife stalks Jacqueline as she walks home along a dark, city street.

4. A sickly young woman introduces herself to Jacqueline: "I'm Mimi. I'm dying" and a few minutes later—as a narrator reprises Donne's doleful lines of poetry—we watch Mimi slowly descending a staircase to enjoy, if she can, one last night on the town before abandoning herself to the illness that is killing her.

This final scene is profoundly shocking, though not in any way a midnight movie audience would recognize. Many miss the ending's impact because it hinges on a subtle, off-camera effect: the sound of a chair falling over—a signal that a major character has committed suicide by hanging. The deadly hush of defeatism that has tinged the entire film has now totally enveloped it.

The Seventh Victim is so muted, so poetic, and so serious (despite its somewhat absurd plot) that contemporary audiences raised on such prosaic horror movies as *The Exorcist* and *Rosemary's Baby* are generally unequipped to understand it.* Nor does the film have much to offer academic axe-grinders. Not long ago I caught *The Seventh Victim* at a local university. After the screening the apparently intelligent and reasonable young woman who had introduced it postulated that this delicate and haunting film is, in fact, nothing more than another exhibit in the case against Hollywood and its insidious campaign to stratify women into the polarized negative stereotypes of madonna (Mary) or whore (Jacqueline). Meanwhile I'm kicking myself for forgetting the cardinal rule of attending a college film society screening: Get the hell out of there before the lights go up.

---

*"As an adventure in stylish diabolism," wrote Doug McClelland in his book *The Golden Age of "B" Movies*, *The Seventh Victim* ". . . makes *Rosemary's Baby* look like *Blondie's Blessed Event*."

★

THE BEST
Mechanical-Man Scene

★

In William Saroyan's novel *The Human Comedy* a little boy is scared half to death by a mechanical man advertising health tonic in a store window. A sign identifies the man as MR. MECHANO—THE MACHINE MAN—HALF MACHINE, HALF HUMAN. MORE DEAD THAN ALIVE. $50 IF YOU CAN MAKE HIM SMILE. $500 IF YOU CAN MAKE HIM LAUGH. When I was a boy something similar happened to me in a movie theater, but instead of being frightened I was awestricken—it was, I guess, my first movie epiphany.

City That Never Sleeps, the picture I was watching, is the story of a disenchanted young cop on the brink of quitting the force, leaving his wife, and running off with a stripper named Angel Face to begin a new and possibly crooked life. Angel Face (Mala Powers) is loved by Gregg (Wally Cassell), a failed actor employed as a mechanical man by the Silver Frolics, the joint where Angel Face peels. Hour after hour, night after night, Gregg, decked out in full white-tie regalia, does his robot act in the club's front window while curious passersby try to figure out whether he's a man pretending to be a machine or a machine pretending to be a man. During the course of his degrading duties Gregg becomes the sole witness to a street murder and, knowing the murderer will return to kill him and figuring he has nothing to lose but his wretched life, volunteers to act as a decoy for the police. When he steps into the window to begin his routine, a dark wave of pre-Felliniesque magic engulfs the movie. As the killer watches undercover across the street, Angel Face, moved by Gregg's sad courage, speaks to him from the wings of his little stage, telling him she wants to straighten out and have a good life: "I want to dream like you . . . of the beautiful things". She has decided to accept his standing offer to quit the club and join him in a husband-and-wife comedy act. Cut to a giant close-up of a tear rolling down Gregg's metallic-painted face. "Harry, Harry, look!" exclaims a tipsy spectator to her escort. "The mechanical man is crying!" A shot rings out and the window shatters.

It is never made entirely clear whether Gregg escapes unharmed, although he appears to, and whether he and Angel Face follow their dream and start a new life together (they're only a subplot), but I've always hoped that he does and that they do.

★

THE BEST

Musical Moment in a Nonmusical Movie

★

Rock-and-roll dancing is generally unwatchable; who wants to look at someone else "do his own thing"? An exception is the Madison, a precision dance that can be quite beautiful. Like other rock-and-roll dances the Madison is unilateral; no one touches or even looks at anyone else— unlike the others, however, it's done in sync; even if Madison dancers haven't rehearsed, each, at least, knows the formula.

Midway through the French New Wave gem *Band of Outsiders* three overgrown waifs are seated in a café planning their first robbery. One of them is Anna Karina (Odile), an actress whose radiant beauty and emotive catalog recall the great movie stars of the silent era; the other two are Sami Frey (Franz) and Claude Brasseur (Arthur). Franz gets up to play the jukebox. Odile and Arthur follow him. Franz places his black felt gangster's hat on Odile's head; it goes well with her dark sweater, tartan skirt, and black stockings. Standing side by side, Odile in the middle, the trio proceed to do a very cool, clean, and guardedly lighthearted version of the Madison (finger snap, hand clap, hop stomp, forward shuffle, right face, left face, sidestep) with near perfect precision. Periodically the music stops (but not the sounds of the finger snapping, hand clapping, and foot stamping) to allow the voice of the film's director, Jean-Luc Godard, to reveal the dancers' thoughts: "Arthur kept looking at his feet, thinking of Odile's romantic kisses . . . Odile wonders if the two boys see her breasts move under her sweater . . . Franz is wondering if the world is a dream or a dream is the world." Finally the boys tire and they peel off the screen leaving Odile doing a solo until she too stops. Among the cinema's great privileged moments, this lovely interlude of (narratively) impromptu but (actually) nonspontaneous fun (it was rehearsed for two weeks) leads me to the subversive suspicion that most of the best potential of movies lies hidden in the white spaces of their scripts.

★

THE BEST
Version of *Carmen*

★

The story of Carmen has been brought to the screen many times, in versions starring Geraldine Farrar, Theda Bara, Pola Negri, Dolores del Rio, Viviane Romance, and Rita Hayworth, among others. In addition to these more or less traditional interpretations, the *Carmen* canon has been expanded to include a Chaplin spoof (with Edna Purviance as Carmen and Charlie as "Darn Hosiery"), a "jazz" Carmen (*Carmen Jones* with Dorothy Dandridge), a soft-core smut version (*Carmen Baby*), and a far-afield, modern-day makeover by Jean-Luc Godard (the wonderfully titled *First Name: Carmen*). The fact that I have seen none of the above—nor Francesco Rosi's full-blown 1984 adaptation of the Bizet opera—does not for a moment deter me from declaring the heavyweight champion *Carmen* of all time to be the 1983 Spanish dance version directed by Carlos Saura and choreographed by Antonio Gades. Like *The Tales of Hoffmann* and *French Cancan*, the Saura-Gades *Carmen* is one of those rare musical movies that instantly involve and eventually enthrall you with the elegance of their conceptions, the assuredness of their executions, and the inexorability of their rhythms.

The film's tension operates on three levels of (un)reality. Inside the smallest of three Chinese boxes is the story of a hot-blooded Gypsy girl whose allure and perfidy destroy the soldier sent to arrest her. This is the plot of the work we watch being rehearsed by the dance company led by the character played by Antonio Gades. The movie's second level of meaning surfaces when the Gades character begins a love affair with the dancer he has chosen to portray Carmen; the name of this dancer is also Carmen and she is played by the dancer-actress Laura Del Sol. This obsessive liaison lays the groundwork for a framing story which closely parallels the scenario of the dance work being rehearsed. A third level of meaning is implied in the fact that several members of the film's cast seem to be playing themselves: Antonio, a dancer-choreographer who is preparing a stage version of *Carmen*, is played by Antonio Gades, a dancer-choreographer whose production of *Carmen* indeed was performed in theaters following the release of the film; guitarist-composer Paco is played by guitarist-composer Paco de Lucia; and Cristina, the troupe's principal female dancer is played by Cristina Hoyos, who plays the same role in real life. (In the real-life stage production Hoyos was cast as Carmen, a part she is considered too old to play in the production we see being prepared in the movie.) Follow? (I have no idea, by the way, whether Mr. Gades and Miss Del Sol carried this concentric symmetry to its logical conclusion by having an off-screen affair, though I happily am able to assure you that Miss Del Sol remains alive and well to this day.)

The first thing to impress me in this film was its basic set: a vast, bare, clean, modern dance studio with one massive glass wall looking out not on a sweaty Seville but on a crisp, wintry suburban landscape; I immediately fell in love with this set and its inhabitants, a close-knit band of show people whose obvious camaraderie and unassuming professionalism render them entirely appealing. Just as the cold landscape contrasts with the warm interior of the studio, these attractive young (and not so young) moderns contrast with the primitive poseurs who comprise the personae of the story of Carmen. Modern as they may be, however, they are not entirely immune to the ancient passions.

The movie's first big sequence is the rehearsal of the fight in the factory, a highly dramatic and compelling ensemble dance set solely to the sounds of the feet, hands, and voices of the company; it is here that one first receives intimations that some of the players in this show within a show may be beginning to lose themselves in their parts, though there is as yet no concrete basis for this suspicion beyond the intensity of the performances. Most of the film's remaining musical passages prove to be comparatively brief or fragmentary, though we're never more than minutes away from music (the film's score is an inspired combination of Bizet and the folk-informed themes of Paco de Lucia) or dance (an especially exciting a cappella dance interlude is provided by the ensemble being drilled by the voice of Antonio, as, their feet captured in traveling close-up, they stomp back and forth across the studio floor).* In another brilliant scene Saura and Gades momentarily break the incredible tension they've been building by staging "The Toreador's Song" as a farcical bullfight ad-libbed by members of the company during a birthday party; it is here that the mutual affection within the group is most apparent. Throughout, Saura stuffs the cracks between the movie's peak moments of performance and drama with a fascinating series of behind-the-scenes behavioristic observations.

A major conceptual turning point occurs late in the movie: Antonio is involved in what appears to be a friendly card game with (the dancer) Carmen's dope-dealer husband, Montoya; Antonio accuses Montoya of cheating, Montoya slams the surface of the table with his cane, and the two square off to fight; but instead of fighting . . . they *dance*—and the film slips over the boundary between the ostensibly real and the illusory.

*When my mother and I attended a screening of *Carmen* in the 2,400-seat auditorium of a Boca Raton college, at the conclusion of this dance one-sixth of the audience, an old man, shouted "Bravo!"

Cut to the finale, where we find ourselves observing: a dress rehearsal? a party for cast and crew? a festival? a fantasy lodged in Antonio's possibly diseased mind? We see a matador dressing for the ring. After he makes a few practice passes with his cape, a large, black curtain parts to reveal a wall-length mirror, in front of which the entire cast and crew of the company materialize and pair off to enjoy some spirited social dancing. Among the dancing couples are Antonio/Don José and Carmen/Carmen. The matador appropriates Carmen for a dance, Antonio pulls her back, the two men exchange drop-dead looks, then the matador and his clique do some don't-tread-on-me finger snapping and retreat. As someone sings a song about love and jealousy, the collective dancing resumes and we see Antonio and Carmen squabbling. Carmen leaves Antonio to join the matador. Antonio reclaims her for a second time. Knives are drawn and brandished. The finger snapping begins again, this time supplemented by hand clapping, foot stamping, and singing. Antonio accepts the matador's challenge and begins a confrontational dance. As the music track sounds the final duet from Bizet's opera, Carmen storms off, Antonio follows and overtakes her, they argue, he repeatedly attempts to embrace her, and she repeatedly rebuffs him. Finally, he pulls out a knife and stabs her three times, she falls dead at his feet, and the camera pulls away from them and to the side to fix on a sunlit area of the studio where people are sitting in groups and relaxing, unaware of the crime of passion that has just been committed a few yards away. It's as if the act hadn't taken place at all or had occurred in some other time and some other place, long ago and far away.

The best movie version of *Carmen?* Hell, this was the best movie of the 1980s.

★

THE BEST
Pre-code Lingerie

★

—belongs to Virginia Bruce in *Winner Take All,* but as I'm too much the gent to describe it, and wasn't able to unearth a photo, you'll have to see the movie or take my word for it.

★

THE BEST
Surprise Ending

★

A superbly poignant mixing of English middle-class gentility with pure horror, *Dead of Night* has an ending so ingenious, so exhilarating (James Agee called it "one of the most successful blends of laughter, terror, and outrage that I

Mervyn Johns and Hugo

can remember") that it cried out never to be used again (a cry that the makers of *The Night of the Following Day* unfortunately did not heed). So as not to spoil the fun for future "Dead-Heads," I shall reveal *Dead of Night*'s ending upside down: The film begins with a man driving down a country road and stopping at a large house where he is escorted inside. Apart from a strange feeling of déjà vu, he has no idea why he has come here. In the parlor a group of people take turns telling him of supernatural experiences they have undergone or heard about. Ultimately, frightening characters from the stories he's been told materialize and join each other in pursuing the protagonist through the house. He is about to strangle someone to death when:

we see him suddenly sit bolt upright in his bed. When his wife suggests that a quiet drive in the country might help rid him of the terrifying dreams he's been having, a puzzled look appears on his face. We last see him driving down the same country road and stopping at the same large house where he is again escorted inside—and as the end credits roll we realize that our hero is living in a perpetual-motion nightmare.

★

THE BEST
Concert Movie

★

The grandaddy of all concert movies, and still the best, was a documentary of the 1958 Newport Jazz Festival made (with the invaluable assistance of editor Aram Avakian) by Bert Stern, a leading high-fashion photographer who infused his film with everything that's appealing about fashion photography (the sensational colors, the ingenious compositions, the great-looking people) and excluded everything unappealing (the snobbism, the decadence, the commercialism). You don't have to like jazz (I don't) to like *Jazz on a Summer's Day*, but it helps to like movies. Like the best fiction films and unlike most documentaries, *Jazz* is a handsome and carefully wrought artifact—and of all the concert movies I've seen (I could never bring myself to see *Woodstock*), it is the most cinematic.

The picture begins in near abstraction with a series of multicolored credits superimposed on the reflection-dappled surfaces of Narragansett Bay and accompanied by "The Train and the River," a classic jazz composition that more than lives up to its lyrical, evocative title. Following the credits we cut to saxist Jimmy Guiffre and his trio performing the number at one of the festival's daytime sessions. It's the movie's first peak sequence and the first in a redoubtable string of immac-

ulately photographed performances, broken up with a delightful assortment of audience-reaction shots and separated by
bits and pieces of local Newport color, among them the
America's Cup trials being held concurrent with the festival.
(In a series of stunning aerial shots of the boat races, the
shimmering surface of the sunlit bay looks like acres of blue
rippled wax.)

The film's second high point is reached when Anita O'Day
takes the stage to proffer frisky, rapid-fire renditions of
"Sweet Georgia Brown" and "Tea for Two." Splendorously
decked out in white gloves, spike heels, and a sleeveless navy
blue sheath dress with white feathered trim, O'Day—as fresh
and pretty as the picture hat that frames her ruddy, toothy
face—totally conquers the crowd (including a young father
the camera discovers bouncing his tot on his knee during the
appropriate passage of "Tea for Two")—or most of them at
least (one young spectator remains irrevocably immersed in
her paperback edition of *Camille*).

Next, we crash a lively party in an old Newport house
where we observe young couples dancing on the roof, kissing
in the windows, and smoking and drinking like crazy while
children frolic in a small amusement park outside. In the attic
of another old building we find Chico Hamilton's shirtless
cellist putting in some practice time; a tight camera shot
makes the smoke from his cigarette appear to be emanating
from the bowing of his instrument. The interlude concludes
with the image of a young partygoer who's had a little too
much fun, staggering toward the twilight shoreline as night
falls on Newport.

The second and only slightly less impressive half of the

film, the evening sessions, begins with George Shearing on piano, bathed in red light, bobbing and weaving and grinning and looking startlingly like a blissed-out Dr. Strangelove.* Next up, Dinah Washington, looking super, does a catchy rendition of "All of Me"; between vocals she helps out Terry Gibbs on the vibes. Washington is followed by Gerry Mulligan and then by Big Maybelle, a traditional, no-nonsense blues shouter who has her audience dancing in the aisles. Now occurs the movie's low point (and the only reason I paid to see it back in 1959): Chuck Berry doing "Sweet Little Sixteen." My hero, as it turned out, was the victim of a lethargic and rather patronizing backup band consisting, it would appear, of whatever musicians happened to be around at the moment. Don't go away though—the best is yet to come: namely, a Chico Hamilton Quintet number that merges African, Spanish, and mid-eastern strains in a performance made immortal by the sublime fluidity of John Pisano's crescendoing guitar and by Hamilton's hypnotic drumming. The camera, hampered perhaps by logistical limitations, fixes Chico in a tight shot and holds him there; all we see are his intensely concentrated, sweating face, his swiveling shoulders, and the ends of his flying tom-tom sticks beating out a long, endlessly repetitive pattern which he varies only in volume. By number's end, the audience is rapt.

Could anyone follow this? An appearance by Louis Armstrong would be the high point of most music documentaries and it's clearly intended to be the high point of this one—

*Meanwhile, among the gatherers outside the gates, Danny Shea and Bill Simone can be spotted hawking extra tickets they've been saddled with by no-show friends (probably me and Paul Comeau).

Stern top-bills Armstrong and allots him more footage than any other artist—but in the light of what has preceded Armstrong and what soon will follow, Louis is something of an anti- (and pre-)climax. The apex of the Armstrong set is not, in fact, his three numbers—the best of them being the mellow interpretation of "Ol' Rockin' Chair" he shares with a bourbon-voiced Jack Teagarden—but the onstage interview that opens the Armstrong segment of the film. Two highlights: 1. Louis, asked if he's ever run into language problems in the course of his extensive touring abroad, replies, "No, no, I'm the pointingest cat you ever seen in your life." 2. Armstrong recalls an exchange he had with the Pope: "He asked me, 'Say, you got any children?' I say, 'Well, no, Daddy, but we still wailin'.'"

After Armstrong's set the MC says, "Ladies and gentlemen, it is Sunday and it is time for the world's greatest gospel singer, Mahalia Jackson." If he had known what was to follow, he might have dropped the qualifying adjective. Jackson, accompanied only by a pianist, sings two magnificent gospel songs, after which she shrugs self-deprecatingly and shyly confesses to an ecstatic audience, "You make me feel like I'm a star." Then she hushes the crowd and delivers a measured, superbly phrased, and incomparably powerful rendition of "The Lord's Prayer." When she's done, a blue credit appears across her massive body and smiling face: END OF A SUMMER'S DAY.

Along with the films of Les Blank, *Jazz on a Summer's Day* is one of the few nonfiction movies that are essentially celebratory rather than didactic; everyone in *Jazz*—the performers, the filmmakers, the Newport audiences—seems to be having a wonderful time. This party atmosphere may explain in part why *Jazz* does not loom large in documentary textbooks—the sheer amount of cigarettes consumed on screen is alone enough to discredit it among the rather puritanical and righteous types who occupy the cinema's nonfiction wing. To the documentarian mind, it would seem, real people don't have fun.

★

THE BEST

Version of the Faust Legend (Incorporating Best Devil, Best Heaven, and Best Resurrection of an Old Joke)

★

In the 1967 comedy *Bedazzled*, Dudley Moore—hopelessly in love with Eleanor Bron, who couldn't care less—sells his soul to the Devil, Peter Cook, in exchange for seven wishes, each of which Cook grants but manages to undermine by slyly injecting a loophole into its scenario: (Wish #2)

Moore is married to Bron, but she's hot for everyone but him; (Wish #5) Bron's mad about him but is married to his best friend (incarnated by Cook), a man so saintly that the guilt-ridden, frustrated lovers find themselves totally incapable of cuckolding him; (Wish #6) Moore and Bron are in love with each other and unattached, but Cook has trapped them both in the bodies of nuns sworn to vows of silence and chastity; and so on.

Peter Cook is a highly attractive and personable Mephistopheles—a glib, breezy chap one feels privileged to accompany as he blithely goes about his daily rounds, which include clipping off the collar buttons of dress shirts, ripping out the last pages of mystery novels, and scoring factory-fresh LPs with an awl (one of which shows up on Moore's turntable at the key moment of a romantic tryst he's sharing with Bron).

Accessible by an up elevator which opens on an idyllic meadow, *Bedazzled*'s Heaven is a spacious and beautiful white greenhouse structured like an elegant chateau. Under its glass dome exotic flora of every variety abide not with worms and insects but with the voice of God.

Midway through Moore's second wish-come-true we find ourselves in the game room of his stately country mansion. A young businessman (Peter Cook again) is playing billiards with one Lord Dowdy, a world-class stutterer. Between shots, Cook complains about market trends. "Sh-sh-sh-surely," sputters Dowdy, "i-i-i-it-it-it-it's only a--t-t-t-te-temporary--s-s-setback." Peter, who's been patiently waiting out his lordship's remark, replies, without batting an eye, "That's very easy for you to say, Lord Dowdy . . ."

As if all this weren't enough, *Bedazzled* includes among its cast of characters hilariously congruous personifications of each of the Seven Deadly Sins. Guess which one Raquel Welch plays.

★

THE BEST
Twist on the King Arthur Legend

★

In a recent book called *Produced and Abandoned*, several of America's top film critics cited and celebrated nearly one hundred outstanding but neglected movies of the past twenty years or so. The book missed a few small boats (and caught a few leaky ones), but it was guilty of only one mortal sin: the omission of George Romero's *Knightriders*. Ostensibly little more than a two-and-a-half-hour "exploitation movie" (the exploitee being the '70s fad for Renaissance fairs) with a tacky "high-concept" premise (*Knightriders*' knights joust on motorcycles, not steeds), the film was generally dismissed, by those who were aware of it at all, as the longest drive-in movie ever made. Directed by Romero in 1981, thirteen years after *Night of the Living Dead*, *Knightriders*, though it manifests little of the earlier film's dark poetry, by now should have accumulated comparable cultist credits. But it hasn't; it's the Classic That Never Was. A close-knit band of men and women travel from town to town staging medieval fairs. The high point of each day's activities is a series of jousting contests between knights on lightweight motorcycles. The group's young leader is Billy Davis, a modern-day King Arthur in whom the courage and idealism of his historical counterpart is seasoned with a trace of twentieth-century neuroticism. If Billy is noble and selfless ("I'm not trying to be a hero! I'm fighting the dragon!"), he is also unabashedly unrealistic and unyielding; in the movie's first big confrontational scene, he refuses, against the urgings of his court, to grease the palm of a crooked local cop, because "it's *wrong* to pay this guy off." His absolutism and moral recalcitrance eventually lead him to the edge of a nervous breakdown ("It's real hard to live for something you believe in")—and when a combination of hard times and the insidious intrusions of crass promotional types break up and scatter the troupe, Billy goes into retreat to wait for his "stray sheep" to return, against all odds, to the fold.

Knightriders, oddly enough, is weakest in its action sequences, the very elements, one assumes, that got the project financed in the first place; the idea of knights jousting on motorcycles talks better than it plays. What impresses most is the drama inherent in the movie's moral conflicts and in the various ways its characters play out their struggles with each other, with the outside world, and with themselves. In his first starring role, Ed Harris is magnificent as Billy; Harris's virile portrayal of this anachronistic Arthur, this Knight of the Living Dead, reflects the same sort of charismatic authority and high seriousness that made the early performances of Marlon Brando and Steve McQueen so powerful. Tom Savini, a small but spectacularly sinister-handsome man, gives a very amusing performance as Billy's rival, Morgan, a character torn between the impulsions of his personal ambitiousness and innate irreverence ("I was never into this King Arthur crap. I was into the bikes, man") and something maddeningly, elusively seductive about Billy's crackpot crusade.

The best straight version of the King Arthur legend is Robert Bresson's *Lancelot du Lac*, but *Knightriders* is the most original and inspiring spin-off. I defy anyone to sit through its final sequence—a mythologically reverberant reel comparable in content and impact to the conclusions of Sam Peckinpah's *Ride the High Country* and Jean-Pierre Melville's *Le Samourai*— without being swept up in it. *Sure*, it's a movie created essentially for adolescent boys, but at least it's not an ugly, stupid, corrupt movie created for adolescent boys (you know the kind of picture I'm talking about; the malls are full of them).

★

THE BEST
Theme Song

★

There's something about a zither that can make an ordinary tune sound seductively sad and a bittersweet melody (like "It Might as Well Be Spring") sound deeply, deliciously melancholy. This is why you rarely hear "The Third Man Theme" played on a guitar or a piano; at heart just a dumb little ditty, it needs a zither to transform it into the plaintive melody that has haunted moviegoers for forty years. We owe it all to Anton Karas, who adapted and, in an early example of multitrack recording, performed *The Third Man*'s innovative, all-zither score. The film opens on a close-up of a zither with its frame cropped out of the picture—all we see are the instrument's strings and its sound hole. We hear the zither being played, but we can't see the fingers that are making its strings vibrate. Superimposed on the strings, like notes on a staff, the movie's credits begin to appear, and when Karas's credit arrives, the music rises in pitch and intensity like the barking of a pup celebrating his master's return. One of the biggest hit songs of its time, "The Third Man Theme," through no fault of its own, almost single-handedly gave birth to the notion that every movie must come equipped with its own potentially chart-topping theme song—a monumentally bum idea that dogs us to this day.

In case you're wondering, this is the last *Third Man* entry in this book—though the film could be cited additionally under Best English Movie, Best Selznick Production, Best Graham Greene Adaptation, and Best Balloon Man (pre-Fellini).

★

THE BEST
Suspense Thriller

★

Four men are charged with trucking 200 gallons of nitroglycerine over 300 miles of bad road. The smallest jolt could blow them all to hell . . .

That is the premise of *The Wages of Fear*, the second of three masterpieces of misanthropy directed by Frenchman Henri-Georges Clouzot. The first, *Le Corbeau* (1943), was a ruthless dissection of creeping social malignancy in a small provincial town. Financed by a German film company and allegedly exhibited as Nazi propaganda under the damning microcosmic title *A French Village*, *Le Corbeau* won Clouzot a top spot on the French film industry's blacklist until 1947. *Les Diaboliques*, the most commercial of the three films, was a horror-thriller released in 1955 to enormous popular acclaim. In between "The Crow" and "The Crones" came *The Wages of Fear*, which hit the festival trail in 1953 and knocked Europe for a loop, winning Best Film awards at Cannes, at Berlin, and from the British Film Academy. Said *Variety* at the time: "Cast presence of Yves Montand, and publicity agent his Commie leanings presents a problem for its possible U.S. market. Director Clougot (sic) is also reportedly far on the left side." And somewhat ominously: "Trimming is needed to get this down to a more digestible size." The film's U.S. distributors were not about to back down before *Variety*'s challenge; when the picture opened here in 1955 it was missing more than twenty percent of its original two and a half hours of footage. Thirty-six years later the film was restored to full or nearly full length (there may be a few fragments missing still) and the restored material greatly enhances what had been a compelling work even in its abridged form.

The value of the 1991 reconstruction lies primarily in its reestablishment of the balance between the movie's two basic movements: The Town and The Road (the here and the gone). Most of the restored footage turns up in the film's first and less renowned section, a beautifully sustained hour of character establishment, local color, and thematic loomings. Here we are introduced to an uncomely assortment of Huston-esque have-nots as they lie moldering in the bars and barrens of a squalid Latin American village, unable to score enough work to finance their escapes back to the various corners of Europe they came from. Sick with boredom, alienation, nostalgia for home, and encroaching starvation, they have fallen into the patterns of petty territorialism and ritualistic machismo characteristic of idle men thrown together in hopeless

Vera Clouzot and Yves Montand

situations. It's a measure of Clouzot's misanthropy that hardly a one of these down-and-out out-of-towners furnishes us with even a hint that he'd be anything but a minor-league loser anywhere else. One day, four of our (anti)heroes are offered a priceless but potentially deadly ticket to ride.

It's the bedrock of these first six reels that make the knuckle-whitening suspense to come so rich and resonant; every sequence, every scene, every shot contributes to and dignifies the subsequent action. Two outstanding early sequences: 1. A pair of louts engage each other in a bluff-and-counterbluff battle for control over the atmosphere of a crummy little café; 2. A veteran vagrant educates a newcomer in the harsh realities facing foreigners in this village—said initiation taking the form of a two-minute-real-time conversation that has been cinematically redistributed over a period of probably hours and possibly days as it transpires first in a café and then, respectively, on a rooftop (complete with buzzards), at an airline ticket window, outside an unfinished and abandoned building, under shelter from a torrential tropical rainstorm, and finally from within the funeral procession of a fellow European. Filmmakers have employed this device since and probably before Clouzot but too often to no purpose beyond a desperate and misguided desire to "open up" the scene at hand. Clouzot uses it to define both a world and a climate of the soul.

It is in the second section of *Wages*, the deadly trek, that the justly celebrated suspense takes over, enriched by perhaps the only sustained passage of human tenderness in a mature Clouzot work, as the truck drivers' common bonds of hope and dread bring them to the brink of camaraderie and mutual affection. One of many splendid moments: A man rolling himself a smoke is alerted to an enormous but distant explosion by the split-second disappearance of tobacco from the cigarette paper he is holding.

The Wages of Fear was considered rather strong stuff in the mid-'50s (though not strong enough to prevent audiences from flocking to it in record numbers). In the disaffected days of the present, its unremitting pessimism seems easier to take, while its "controversial" elements—some homosexual undertones and an unflattering portrayal of an American oil company—now seem almost innocuous. (Karel Reisz called the film "admittedly anti-American" but only as part and parcel of being "unselectively and impartially anti-everything.") If our parents found *Wages*' contents on the gamy side, our children may someday find them positively quaint. Changing reactions to the film's *formal* values, on the other hand, may well follow a reverse pattern. It's become almost an axiom of modern life that the more sophisticated technology grows, the crasser become the sensibilities controlling it; if you want to know what "overkill" means, check out any sci-fi, horror, cop, or FX thriller currently oozing out of Hollywood. Thus, if *Wages* has lost a half step in the morbidity marathon, it's gained a step in the cineastic sweepstakes; in comparison with current product, *Wages* looks even better than it did in 1955, a year which also marked the release of *Kiss Me Deadly*, *The Night of the Hunter*, *The Big Knife*, *Rebel Without a Cause*, *The Big Combo*, *East of Eden*, among others. It was a lot less lonely at the top back then.

Expertly written, directed, photographed, and edited, *The Wages of Fear* is a bit uneven in the acting department, though its viewers are not likely to soon forget Yves Montand, virile and laconically attractive as a Corsican who's down on his luck, or Vera (Mme H-G) Clouzot, erotically memorable (she looks like your sixth-grade teacher on aphrodisiacs) as a tarty townie with an extra-Clouzotian heart—and for once one is grateful for the stereotype—of gold. All in all, Clouzot's finest movie stands with Robert Bresson's *A Man Escaped*, two or three Jean-Pierre Melville films, and very few others as a personal yet perfectly crafted work that is as superbly entertaining as it is artistically advanced; like the Bresson masterpiece, *Wages* is an escape film that is far from escapist fare. From the opening pre-Peckinpah image of a child overseeing his slave empire of beetles, to the final, delicious, Huston-like irony (set to the "Blue Danube Waltz"), *The Wages of Fear* stakes its claim as the most exhilarating and strangely satisfying feel-bad movie ever made.

★

THE BEST
Coda

★

Along with John Ford, Raoul Walsh was one of Hollywood's richest and most fertile fonts of Irish-Americana. *The Strawberry Blonde*, one of Walsh's best films, is the story of Biff Grimes (James Cagney), an Irish immigrant laborer's son, who falls in love with a Gay Nineties strawberry-blonde beauty named Virginia (Rita Hayworth), only to lose her to his best friend and partner, Hugo (Jack Carson), who compounds this betrayal by engineering a shady business deal for which Biff is forced to take the rap. The movie is a marvel of shifting moods, jumping back and forth from comedy to romance to drama to farce with enviable assurance—for example: Biff's five-year prison stretch, which is covered in a mere two minutes of screen time and is rendered almost as farce, is followed immediately by a long, poignant scene in which an older, wiser, and wearier Biff, fresh out of jail, returns to his commensurately deflated wife, Amy (Olivia de Havilland) and they quietly, almost shyly reaffirm their commitment to each other as the sound track plays "When You Were Sweet Sixteen." The movie's central song is "And the Band Played On"—the old favorite about a fellow named Casey and his strawberry blonde. The song makes its most memorable appearance in a dance-hall scene in which Biff bribes the house tenor to replace "Casey" with "Biff Grimes" in the song's lyrics while Biff waltzes his own strawberry blonde, Virginia, around the floor.

Someone at Warners must have sensed that the film's audiences, high on a mixture of multifarious emotions, would be reluctant to let go of this captivating movie, so after the story's conclusion we are given a special bonus. A card appears on the screen, nickelodeon style, to announce, in jaunty antique lettering: ONE MOMENT PLEASE! THE MANAGEMENT HAS HAD A GOODLY NUMBER OF REQUESTS FROM OUR GOLDEN VOICED PATRONS ASKING THAT EVERYBODY HERE JOIN IN SINGING 'AND THE BAND PLAYED ON'. ALL RIGHT FOLKS, LET'S GO! Here ensues a series of illustrated sing-along cards—accompanied by an off-screen band and a tenor who sings two choruses of the song (in the second chorus, Biff Grimes's name is again substituted for Casey's)—followed by a final card, THANK YOU . . . COME AGAIN (illustrated with a gent taking a bow), and the last thing we see, as the band plays on, are the players' credits.

I first met and fell in love with *The Strawberry Blonde* in Boston's Brighton Tap, where, once upon a time, one could sit in a booth and enjoy a few beers and a bit of supper while watching two or three old movies projected in 16mm. I'd like to report that the Tap's Irish regulars sang along with *The Strawberry Blonde*'s coda, but I don't recall that they did.

★

THE BEST
Opening Shot

★

Orson Welles's *Touch of Evil* opens with a shot that is so ingenious, complex, and arresting it makes other examples of single-shot filmmaking look primitive in comparison. (Superimposed on this extraordinary shot/scene/sequence, against Welles's wishes, are the movie's main titles.) The shot begins with a close-up of a man's hands holding a time bomb. He sets the dial for three minutes (almost precisely the amount of time remaining in this opening shot) and the bomb begins to tick. The man hears laughter to the left and his body swings in that direction accompanied by Russell Metty's camera, which picks up a distant couple walking toward us through an arcade, then turning east and disappearing behind the far side of a one-story, open-ended liquor market. The camera moves east as well, tracking along the market's parallel wall upon which we see the bomber's shadow racing toward an open white convertible parked in back. Bomber plants bomb in the car's trunk and disappears as laughing couple enter screen left and get in automobile. Car starts up and turns west into same hidden street couple has just traversed as camera, now looking down from a high angle, reverses its path and tracks west across rooftop of liquor mart until it picks up convertible emerging and turning south onto main street of town. We appear to be in the dimly lit downtown area of a small Latin American city (actually, this sequence was shot in Venice, California). Camera is now traveling backward in advance of convertible, which stops to allow pedestrians to cross as camera continues south. Car catches up with camera, then stops for a new pair of pedestrians crossing east to west. The descending camera approaches and follows walking couple, whom we can now identify as Charlton Heston in dark makeup and Janet Leigh, as they continue on their way west through thickening traffic, the walking couple sometimes overtaking and sometimes being overtaken by the couple in the white convertible. Eventually both couples converge at a police checkpoint where two customs cops engage Heston and Leigh in conversation. Here we learn that Heston and Leigh are married, she is an American, and he is a well-known antinarcotics official of some kind. Papers in order, Heston and Leigh exit frame as convertible also clears customs and proceeds from one country into the next. As convertible exits left we hear the glossy blonde inside complaining worriedly, "I got this ticking going through my head." Camera relocates Heston and Leigh (partially obscured behind a series of looming pedestrians heading every which way) still walking west and finally coming to a stop so that Heston can remind Leigh that he hasn't kissed her in over an hour.

He is in the process of making up for lost time when he, she, and we hear a loud explosion. Heston and Leigh took up in alarm and here occurs the first edit in the film as it cuts to an automobile being blown to bits.

Words are incapable of adequately describing the sophistication of this historic exercise in spatial architecture or fully capturing its excitement; it's the kind of thing that makes youngsters want to become filmmakers and makes established filmmakers want to retire in envy and frustration.

★

THE BEST
Speech

★

"I'm sorry, but I don't want to be an emperor—that's not my business. I don't want to rule or to conquer anyone. I should like to help everyone, if possible—Jew and Gentile, Black, White . . ."

It is near the end of *The Great Dictator*. Due to his uncanny resemblance to the führer, a little Jewish barber, played by Charlie Chaplin, finds himself in the dire position of having to address a huge fascist rally. After a certain amount of comic fumbling, the little barber rises to his feet and—speaking in a rapid crescendo with very little inflection—delivers the noblest speech in film history, a three-minute harangue in which he asks, urges, pleads with his audience to "fight for a new world, a decent world that will give men a chance to work, that will give youth a future and old age a security . . . Let us fight to free the world, to do away with national barriers, to do away with greed, with hate and intolerance." The problem is that it's not the uneducated, semiarticulate barber who speaks to us but Chaplin himself. In doing so he vandalizes his own film and undermines its artistic integrity . . . or so goes the conventional wisdom. But what does conventional wisdom know about unconventional genius? Film critic Jonathan Rosenbaum defied the former when he wrote of the speech's "total inadequacy . . . as art, as thought, as action, as anything" and then proceeded to eloquently defend and justify it: "Seen with historical hindsight, there are few moments in film as raw and convulsive as this desperate coda. Being foolish enough to believe that he can save the world, Chaplin winds up breaking our hearts in a way no mere artist ever could . . . Chaplin doesn't really belong to the history of cinema; he belongs to history."

★

THE BEST

Gingerless
Fred Astaire Duet

★

If you've seen Fred Astaire and Eleanor Powell dance to "Begin the Beguine" in *That's Entertainment!* or TV compilations, you've seen the best of it, but you haven't seen the half of it; in its original context, *Broadway Melody of 1940*, the number is a full-blown, four-part, nine-minute extravaganza. Part One opens in an orchestra pit with a sultry, saronged beauty singing a standard romantic arrangement of the Cole Porter tune; surrounding her are a similarly clad singing chorus, lounging around on some plush, white, not very functional looking upholstery. After a few phrases of the song, the camera cranes up to the stage and a scrim curtain sweeps open on a night of tropical splendor, dominated by a starlit backdrop darkly reflected in a mirrored floor; several palm trees; and a mounded platform, center stage, upon which a multitude of matching dancing girls seem to be swaying. From behind this raised area looms a bare-midriffed Eleanor Powell, dressed in an abbreviated bolero jacket, a tassled bra, and a long, wispy skirt. Powell does some of her patented high kicks and knuckle-bruising back bends; then the chorus exits and a subtle camera movement introduces

into the background of the frame a mirrored wall in which we
see the small figure of Fred Astaire in short jacket and high-
waisted trousers. Part Two: Powell advances toward Fred's
reflection until eventually the real Fred enters the frame
behind her and joins her in a syncopated tap-flamenco duet,
their light-toned, whirling images reflected in the blackness
of the mirrored floor. ("Begin the Beguine," along with "In
the Still of the Night," from the same movie, is one of the
best-looking black-and-white numbers Hollywood ever
filmed.) It's all quite beautiful and elegant but a touch
reserved, a bit formal; the best is still to come.

But not immediately. First a silly quartet of female vocalists
offers a swing arrangement of "Begin the Beguine" (Part
Three); meanwhile, in the mirror behind them, an orchestra's
playing. The quartet departs and the tropical dancing girls
shuffle off to Borneo, but the orchestra continues the swing
"Beguine" as Astaire and Powell, now transformed into Fred
and Eleanor, return, refreshingly costumed in all-American
white, to finish things off (Part Three). They never touch—
the somewhat stately courtship they transacted a few minutes
before has now mellowed into friendship. And what a friendly
dance they do (if anything so exhilarating can be termed
"friendly"): a dynamite display of old-fashioned side-by-side
tap (Eleanor's expressions throughout are priceless) incorporating an inspired interlude of a cappella challenge dancing
conducted less in a spirit of competition than in one of mutual
affection. Midway, they pick up the pace and a climactic
moment divine occurs when, circling each other in an intoxicating succession of spins, they periodically shoot their right
arms out over their heads, first alternately and then simulta-

neously. This was probably the easiest move to execute in the entire routine, but it's a delightfully flashy and nonetheless gratifying one, the sizzle that makes the steak seem tastier. Finally, they stop on a dime, their feet planted firmly on the ground, their arms extended out toward the audience, "Mammy" style. So quickly do they come to a stop and so very precisely, the pleated skirt of Eleanor's dress doesn't finish the dance until a beat or two after she does.

★

THE BEST
Film Noir Wisecrack

★

Double Indemnity, early on, the parlor of Barbara Stanwyck's suburban home, where Fred MacMurray has just encountered her for the first time. There's something about Stanwyck that pegs her as no better than she has to be and potentially a whole lot worse—maybe it's the anklets, maybe it's the ankles, maybe it's the long blond hairdo that looks like it's on loan from Señor Wences, maybe it's the trace of a sneer in her smile. Whatever it is, MacMurray likes it and accordingly switches gears from small talk to sexual innuendo with a series of pitches that Stanwyck almost but not quite fields. Finally Stanwyck pulls up a little short and says, "I wonder if I know what you mean." MacMurray, on his way out the door, replies, "I wonder if you wonder."

★

THE BEST

Man-to-Man Conversation in a Barroom

★

We are midway in *Meet John Doe*, Frank Capra's ambitious, stirring, but somewhat muddled 1941 attack on antidemocratic elements in America. James Gleason plays the hard-nosed editor of a big-city newspaper owned by closet fascist Edward Arnold. Gary Cooper is the gullible young man the paper has chosen to impersonate "John Doe," a bogus character it has created as part of a circulation-boosting stunt. It is a dark and rainy evening. Cooper, on his way to address thousands of John Doe Club members at an outdoor rally, is approached by Gleason, drunk, who invites him into Jim's Bar for a little chat. Gleason, it turns out, does most of the chatting; Cooper confines himself mainly to looking uncomfortable and contributing an occasional "No, sir" or "You betcha."

James Gleason was a Hollywood veteran who specialized in portraying tough-talking, weathered Irishmen. The barroom scene from *Meet John Doe* provided him with a rare opportunity, not to escape type casting but to transcend it. As Otis Ferguson put it, "[Gleason] made more of this chance than there was in the lines and their meaning . . . It was just talk, with business, but he made [the scene] his, and it will remain one of the magnificent scenes in pictures." Belting back shot after shot of whiskey, Gleason reminisces about the First World War and how he and his father had enlisted together and served in the same outfit, how the son had seen the father fall, and how the son survived the war without a scratch. Then, after summoning the waiter, Tubby, for another whiskey, Gleason confesses a soft spot in his hard-boiled shell: "I'm a sucker for this country—I *like* what we got here," and he gets mad, he says, when somebody comes along and tries to foul the nest. Along the way, he invokes the names of Washington, Jefferson, Lincoln—"Lighthouses, John. Lighthouses in a foggy world." Then he tries to tip Cooper off that Arnold has been exploiting Cooper's ingenuousness in order "to shove his way into the White House, so he [can] put the screws on, so he [can] turn out the lights in those lighthouses." Cooper doesn't buy this exposé, not yet anyway. In fact he almost punches Gleason out for his trouble, then storms out of the bar, leaving Gleason alone with his jag and with Tubby. (One wants to take Gleason home at this point, kiss him on his noble brow, and put him to bed.) My favorite lines in this classic scene are Gleason's first: "You're a nice guy, John. I like you. You're gentle. I always liked gentle people. Me? I'm hard. Hard and tough. I got no use for hard people."

There are two other memorable lines in *Meet John Doe*. The first is spoken by Walter Brennan, Cooper's hobo sidekick and the film's designated skeptic: "I know the world's been shaved by a drunken bahba." The second, the movie's final line, is delivered by our old pal Jimmy Gleason above the sound of the choral finale of Beethoven's Ninth: Gleason, all 130 righteous pounds of him, turns to fat cat Arnold and says—well, I'll leave it to you to find out what he says because: 1. The line plays better than it reads, 2. I want you to see the movie, and 3. I've already in this book let several climactic cats out of the bag and I think I may have unbagged my limit.

★

THE BEST
Dickens Adaptation

★

"In the year 1836 Messrs Chapman and Hill, the publishers, paid the vast sum of fourteen pounds a month to a comparatively obscure young journalist of twenty-four years of age to write a series of comic adventures around an imaginary club and the misadventures of its members. His name was Charles Dickens and he obliged by creating the Pickwick Club." So begins Noel Langley's 1954 adaptation of *The Pickwick Papers*, the best film adaptation of a Dickens work and one of the most successful screen adaptations of any literary classic ever. Most Dickens movies are more concerned with telling a Dickens story than capturing the Dickens spirit, and this may explain the episodic *Pickwick Papers'* relative lack of prestige and popularity with a narrative-minded moviegoing public and critical establishment. It's not that *The Pickwick Papers* doesn't get its story told—it does, and with commendable efficiency; it's just that the movie's main order of business is to capture as faithfully as possible Dickens's characters, their times, and their social milieu. An affectionately satiric comic tone is established at the outset and, with one exception, never betrayed. A less assured filmmaker might have shorn the story's romantic and melodramatic moments of their comic foundations in the name of "balance," but in Langley's *Pickwick*, only the scenes in debtor's prison are exempted from the overall comic tone.

There are dozens of speaking roles, each of them impeccably cast, right down to the flighty cook in a girls' boarding school, a character who is on hand for only a few moments. It's difficult to single out for praise any one actor in this memorable ensemble, but Nigel Patrick's performance is so charming, witty, and, ultimately touching, it should be counted among the finest in the English cinema. As I watch this picture, I'm struck by how deeply the great movie comedians of the silent era were indebted to Dickens (and by how much this Dickens adaptation is indebted in turn to them)—or am I imagining the Charlie Chaplin in Nigel

Patrick's Mr. Jingle, the Harry Langdon in James Donald's Mr. Winkle, the Oliver Hardy in Alexander Guage's Mr. Tupman, the Buster Keaton in Harry Fowler's Sam Weller, the Fatty Arbuckle in Gerald Campion's Fat Boy, and the Stan Laurel in Joyce Grenfell's Mrs. Hunter?

The Pickwick Papers is the Merrie Olde England movie *Tom Jones* tried and—due to its misguided and vulgar attempts to ingratiate itself with a "hip" '60s audience—largely failed to be. *Pickwick* is also an ideal if indirect Christmastime story, ending as it does with an unexpected and unmotivated act of charity followed by a Pickwickian toast to "good will, good hope, good nature." Never much of a joiner, I've always considered the idea of the John Doe Clubs of America a trifle disturbing, and the virtues of the Ale and Quail Club best appreciated from a distance, but, despite the Jingle in my soul, I'd gladly raise a toast to the immortal Pickwick Club and its naive, decent, silly, gentle membership.

★

THE BEST
Dirty Joke
Ever Smuggled into a
Hollywood Studio Cartoon

★

Long before a jaded world witnessed Fritz the Cat futzing around with a tubful of frisky female felines, the lads at Warner's Termite Terrace really got away with one.

It is 1943. The cartoon is "An Itch in Time." A dog has just had his most personal parts blown up by TNT (don't ask). In search of relief he proceeds to drag the affected area across the parlor rug, howling as he goes. Midway he freezes, turns to the camera, and says in a rather pleased tone of voice, "Hey, I better cut this out. I may get to like it!"—then immediately picks up his itchy odyssey just where he left off.

★

THE BEST
Movie of All Time

★

I vote for *Les Enfants Terribles*. No, not *Les Enfants du Paradis* but *Les Enfants Terribles*, Jean-Pierre Melville's brilliant adaptation of Jean Cocteau's cult novel about a teenage sister and brother whose obsessive love for each other leads to their mutual downfall. Why is this my favorite movie? Because it is the most successful blending of the classical and romantic traditions I've yet to see on film. Because it anticipated the French New Wave by a full decade. Because its score—perhaps the most exciting example of classical music scoring in the history of the cinema—introduced me to Vivaldi. Because it offers in Nicole Stephane's Elizabeth the most dazzling performance by a woman in film history. And because it answers, better than any other movie, Diaghilev's famous challenge to the young Cocteau: "Astonish me."

Edouard Dhermitte and Nicole Stephane

★

II

PEOPLE

★

Cary Grant and Billy Gilbert in *His Girl Friday*

★

THE BEST
Bit Player

★

Unlike a Claude Rains or an Agnes Moorehead, the Hollywood bit player wasn't allowed the luxury of building a sustained performance over a ninety-minute period but had to make an impression in a matter of minutes lest he be mistaken for a talking extra. Among his/her typical assignments were *Drunk*, *Waitress*, *Cabby*, *Judge*, and *Pretty Girl in Speakeasy*, though he/she frequently had to settle for the even more thankless role of *Cop*, *Bank Teller*, *Desk Clerk*, *Andrew as a Boy*, *Robbery Victim*, *Cleaning Lady*, *Hood*, or *Blonde*. Often the bit player's position in a movie's hierarchy of performers was deducible from the degree to which his billing had been personalized. If he's *Doctor Doxley*, he's a supporting player; if he's *Doctor*, he's a bit.

During his thirty-four-year film career Billy Gilbert was allotted his fair share of supporting roles, the most prestigious being Herring in *The Great Dictator*, and even an occasional co-lead in a B comedy, but he earned his daily bread doing bits—dozens and dozens of bits. *Rosalie*; *Espionage*; *Maytime*; *Sea Devils*; *China Passage*; *The Firefly*; *Captains Courageous*; *Music for Madame*; *On the Avenue*; *Live, Love and Learn*; *We're on the Jury*; *Broadway Melody of 1938*; *Fight for Your Lady*; *When You're in Love*; *The Man Who Found Himself*; *The Outcasts of Poker*

Flat; *The Toast of New York*; *The Life of the Party*; *One Hundred Men and a Girl*—these are the films Gilbert made in 1937 *alone*, with enough time left over to furnish *Snow White and the Seven Dwarfs* with the voice of Sneezy. All told, he appeared in well over one hundred movies (nobody knows the exact number), many of them without billing.

Billy was a large man (280 pounds) but delicate in gesture, and the characters he played were wide of eye and gentle of soul—they would get mad, but they would not get mean. His trademark was his elastic larynx, which gave one the impression of a man talking and snoring at the same time, and he was the actor you'd ask for when looking for a sneeze-and-wheeze specialist. His signature state was one of bulky, blustery, befuddled inefficiency and he varied it with an endless assortment of takes, double takes, and other tics of the trade perfected during his youthful years in burlesque. For Billy at his best see *His Girl Friday*, in which he's been entrusted with not only a name, Joe Pettibone, but two entire scenes. He is still trapped, however, in a classic bit-player vocation; he's a glorified messenger, a low-level civil servant who's one or two mental beats behind everyone he confronts among the sharks and sharpies who comprise the movie's personae. Keep your eye on him throughout his two scenes and you'll discover that he's usually listening not to the character who is speaking at the moment but to the character who has just finished speaking. This hint of retardation in tangent with the overlapping nature of *His Girl Friday*'s astonishingly well-timed dialogue results in perhaps the film's funniest moment: a priceless half second in which Billy concludes that both he and the man he's talking with are named Pettibone.

★

THE BEST
Unbilled Cameo

★

I t occurs at the end of *In the Good Old Summertime*. After an hour and forty minutes of bickering, Judy Garland and Van Johnson have finally, underneath a Christmas tree, come to terms romantically. Flash forward to a public park three or four years later where Judy and Van in their Sunday finest, toddler in tow, are enjoying a carefree spring stroll. They stop for a moment and Van lifts the little girl, who looks a bit like Mommy but nothing like Daddy, into his arms and gives her a kiss as Judy beams. Just before THE END superimposes itself on the shot, we see that the object of Judy and Van's affection is Liza Minnelli. The reason for the touch of petulance in her expression, Liza tells us now, is that no one had remembered to furnish her with panties for her film debut.

★

THE BEST
Producer

★

recently read a book called *Hollywood's Great Unsolved Mysteries* and was disappointed that at no point did it reveal what a producer does. I have a pretty good idea of what a producer *shouldn't* do, however, and that's indulge in creative meddling; memos from the David O. Selznicks now as always are best returned unopened.

After working for Selznick for eight years, a thirty-eight-year-old writer named Val Lewton accepted an offer from RKO, where, during the war years, he went on to produce an extraordinary series of horror movies. (Lewton maintained that RKO had heard he used to write horrible novels and misunderstood "horrible" for "horror.") Though directed and (officially) scripted by others, these creepy quickies were unmistakably the work of one individual and that was Val Lewton, a man whose oeuvre to this day represents the sole argument on behalf of the producer-as-artist notion. Each film in the series was an exemplar of underkill: sober, literate, quiet to the point of hush, and absolutely sincere in its attitude toward its material, all of which may explain Lewton's perpetual neglect by collegiate and camp sensibilities. (One can almost sense the disappointment and resentment in a repertory cinema when the audience realizes that *I Walked with a Zombie* is a good movie.) The only thing lurid about these films was their names—titles that were chosen in advance by public survey, then imposed on Lewton along with miniscule budgets with which to illustrate them. Beyond that, Lewton was given carte blanche—the powers-that-were in the RKO front office (bless them) felt that cheapo chillers weren't worth tampering with.

There are no monsters, either biological or psychological, in Val Lewton movies. In the most poignant of them, those set in contemporary America, we meet instead a series of decent, intelligent, and, for Hollywood, atypically serious middle-classers confronted with mysterious forces they don't understand. (Manny Farber, with more acuity than sensitivity, saw these Lewtonites as "insipidly normal characters, who reminded one of the actors used in small-town movie ads for the local grocery or shoe store.") Lewton's period pieces, though equally hokum-free, are a bit less ingenuous in regard to human evil—they are, after all, set in Europe. *Bedlam*, in particular, has a quality of malaise and elusive but gnawing malignancy rivaled by few other films (among the few: Roger Corman's *The Masque of the Red Death* and H. G. Clouzot's *Le Corbeau*).

Are these movies scary? Well, no, not exactly—though one of the sole permanent chills I've contracted in a movie theater occurred when a strange and uninvited woman in *Cat People* stops a wedding party cold with the words "Mya sestrah?" (my sister); Val Lewton was a poet of the sad not the scary. Here then—for you who like your martinis dry and your terror tempered—is a list of Val Lewton's nine remarkable horror films (in roughly preferential order): *The Seventh Victim, I*

Walked with a Zombie, *The Ghost Ship*, *Bedlam*, *Cat People*, *The Body Snatcher*, *The Leopard Man*, *The Curse of the Cat People*, and *Isle of the Dead*. A note to minimalists: The combined running time of these nine movies is shorter than the time it takes to read your average monstro novel by Stephen King.

★

THE BEST
Smile

★

The screen's most dazzling smile belongs to Deborah Foreman, the very pretty young actress who played the title role in *Valley Girl*; like the Jane Russell pout and the Kirk Douglas sneer, the Foreman smile is so perfect it's almost generic. In *Valley Girl*, however, she trumps with it too early and too often. If Deb ever finds a director who will allow her to unleash her sensational smile only once or twice per film, entire malls may melt.

★

THE BEST
Western Star

★

John Wayne surely was a better all-around actor than Randolph Scott, but Scott was the better, indeed the ultimate *western* actor— a specialist who, unlike Wayne, seemed uncomfortable anywhere but outdoors and out west. Like Wayne, however, Scott never really hit his stride until middle age when his faintly aristo-

Randolph Scott

cratic Virginia voice; striking, hawkish face; and long, straight body combined with a certain core gentleness and an air of unassuming but irreproachable dignity to form an archetype that all boys wanted to emulate and girls, I'm guessing, yearned not to mother but to daughter. Scott is most fondly remembered for the series of seven sparse but remarkably accomplished and moving westerns he made with Budd Boetticher in the 1950s and for his (relatively) bad guy opposite Joel McCrea's (improbably) good guy in *Ride the High Country*. Scott's resonant final line (to a dying McCrea) in that Sam

Peckinpah masterpiece: "I'll see you later." It was Scott's last film.

★

THE BEST
Actor Never to Receive an Oscar Nomination

★

One of Hollywood's most baffling mysteries is why Edward G. Robinson never received an Academy Award nomination for any of his seven dozen screen roles—despite performing such Oscar-worthy services as curing syphilis (once), exposing fugitive Nazis (twice), and allowing his life to be destroyed by slatternly women (countless times). Other great actors (Cary Grant, Orson Welles, Richard Burton) received no (competitive) Oscars, but Robinson never got as much as an Honorable Mention during the half-century of his movie career, a period that saw some 400 male performances nominated. Why? The cynical answer is: because he was talented. Not a bad theory—but even good actors manage to score a nomination somewhere along the way, although often for the wrong performances. Years from now our grandchildren are going to ask us why Greer Garson was given six nominations (and one statuette) but—apart from a special noncompetitive Oscar awarded a few days after his death—Eddie got diddly. Stuck for an answer, I'm going to tell my grandkids this: One day Robinson, mistaking dapper-but-flashy Jack Warner for the studio bookie, tried to place a small bet with him, and Warner avenged himself by failing to push Eddie for an Oscar forever after. Can you think of a better explanation?

★

THE BEST-
Looking Human Being Ever to Appear on a Movie Screen

★

Were God a mere artisan he would have halted production after finishing Esther Williams—those teeth, that skin, those shoulders, that flesh would have told him that his experimental phase, at least, was over. But God is an artist and so he created Cyd Charisse (with the assistance, to be sure, of the MGM makeup department)—he wanted, you see, to add heavenly grace to the formula (not that Esther was awkward; she was merely a little too down-to-earth to be a goddess). None of this mythology is supported by the opening scene of *On an Island with You*, in which a scantily saronged Venus in the form of Esther Williams rises from the waters of a tropical inlet as Ricardo Montalban serenades her. Given superstar Williams's dazzling drenched beauty it's doubtful that 1948 audiences payed much attention to fifth-billed Cyd Charisse, who can be seen jealously observing the Williams-Montalban assignation from behind some shrubbery. Four years later, however, in *Singin' in the Rain*, Cyd would catch everyone's eye; in fact it's safe to say that several million jaws collectively dropped in the spring of 1952 when *Rain* began its reign. Cyd danced but didn't act in the movie, which was OK because she was never a great actress. People used to complain about a certain woodenness, even iciness in her demeanor when she wasn't dancing, but I think this reserved quality actually augmented the contrasting eroticism she expressed so well in her dances—an eroticism enhanced yet tempered by, maybe enhanced *because* tempered by her ballet training and her innate graciousness. Another contributing factor, I feel, to Cyd's enormous allure was the combination of Scotch, Irish, French, English, and American Indian blood in her background—and it doesn't hurt as well to be born in Texas, home state of beautiful women.

In *Singin' in the Rain*'s Broadway Ballet, Charisse is a gangster's moll whom hayseed Gene Kelly yearns for in vain. Kelly's first encounter with Cyd provides us with one of the

musical cinema's most arresting moments: He, sliding on his knees toward the camera, is stopped short by the sight of his hat (suddenly looming in center frame), which is dangling from a green pump, which is fitted to an arched foot, which is attached to a silk-stockinged leg, which in turn is attached to the emerald green-sheathed torso of Cyd Charisse. Cyd, seated, blows smoke through her nostrils(!), smiles slightly, and, hands on hips, extends leg, foot, pump, and hat from three o'clock to around 12:05 where Gene retrieves it. Then she rises from her chair and begins to do the kind of dance customarily performed to encourage men to purchase tickets admitting them to tents. Meanwhile Gene, a victim of culture shock, can do little more than stand there and gape. In a matter of seconds Cyd had caught the attention of the entire world (or, at least, 49.3 percent of it). The following year Cyd would reprise this torrid turn in *The Band Wagon*'s Girl Hunt Ballet, with Astaire filling in for Kelly and tomato red for emerald green.

What Cyd Charisse had that no other dancer had was erotic chic, and this, combined with her obvious taste and talent, is what made her not merely a great performer but an icon. For additional displays of the Charisse chic, see the gymnasium number from *It's Always Fair Weather* (what Cyd does for a knit dress is beyond my powers of discreet description) and the quasi-striptease from *Meet Me in Las Vegas* (Charisse wears clothes so staggeringly well that it's a toss-up whether one hopes she will shed the stunning black lace cocktail dress she's wearing or leave it on).

I don't believe I will provoke many arguments when I assert that Cyd Charisse had the cinema's most beautiful figure (an inadequate word, but "body" is too vulgar and "form" doesn't get the job done). Historians and classical scholars might accuse me of exaggeration, however, were I to suggest that she may be the most beautiful woman who ever lived; I'm aware, of course, that when Paris first saw Helen he didn't have the advantage of seeing her in 1950s 35mm three-strip Technicolor.

★

THE BEST
Second-Banana Villain

★

In the second screen version of Ernest Hemingway's story "The Killers," one of the title roles is played by the redoubtable Lee Marvin. Director Don Siegel, realizing that no one could out-menace Marvin, sent Clu Gulager, as Marvin's young sidekick, off in a different direction—Gulager plays the apprentice hit man with a boyish restlessness and a frightening unpredictability that both complement and reinforce Marvin's implacable style of intimidation. When not being called upon to supplement his partner's menace with muscle, Gulager's gadfly goon amuses himself by playing with the effects of whomever Marvin is terrorizing at the moment: He winds up a toy car, runs it off a shelf, and giggles; he picks up a vase from the desk of a blind woman, removes and smells the flowers, then pours the water out on the desk; he cleans his sunglasses on the hair of a man he and Marvin have cornered in a steam cabinet; he picks up a silent telephone, holds it to his ear, and listens; he socks a woman on the jaw, then plays with her bruises. It's a classic example of a somewhat limited actor making a performance memorable through (meaningfully in-character) "business." There was nothing limited about Lee Marvin, however; he was one of the cinema's most fiercely intelligent actors and this was one of his most mesmerizing performances. Ernest Hemingway's *The Killers* had one more villain up its sleeve—he was enacted, rather poorly, by Ronald Reagan, in his last film. The sight of a future president of the United States—looking much as he would some years later affably welcoming visitors to the Oval Office—slapping Angie Dickinson silly is startling, to say the least.

★

THE BEST
Performance by a Child

★

As a rule, adult actors should be professionals, but child actors should always be amateurs—as was Hayley Mills when she was chosen to play Gillie Evans in *Tiger Bay*, her first movie. Hayley wasn't an actress, she was something much more valuable—a real little girl who happened to be naturally blessed with such an appealing spirit and sensibility that she was able to command an audience's attention with an authority not granted to "professional children." Her Gillie, a spunky child of the Cardiff waterfront, is so uniquely endearing that she unconditionally wins our affection whatever she's up to—whether it's fighting boys, sassing grownups, singing in the church choir, yearning for a gun of her own, or shamelessly lying to authority figures like the police inspector (played by Hayley's dad, John Mills), who's grilling her about a murder she's witnessed. Faced with the thorny and for a child anguishing moral decision of whether to protect the murderer, a young Polish sailor she has befriended, or face up to her social obligations as a citizen, Gillie, in the end, rest assured, does the right thing.

★

THE BEST
Collection of American Voices in One Movie

★

John Huston's *The Red Badge of Courage* offers up a symphony of splendid American regional voices, among them those of Audie Murphy of Kingston, Texas; Bill Mauldin of Mountain Park, New Mexico; Arthur Hunnicutt of Gravelly, Arkansas; Andy Devine of Flagstaff, Arizona; and Royal Dano of New York, New York (apparently the only real Yankee in Huston's Union Army). Most eloquent of all is the voice of John Dierkes ("The Tall Soldier"), an economist-turned-actor whose birthplace I've been unable to determine but I'd guess is somewhere in or near Ohio. You may remember him as the low-ranking villain Alan Ladd blasts off a second-floor landing in *Shane*; it's a movie in which Dierkes doesn't get to say much, but behind those lanky bones and grizzled features lurked a voice of pure American gold. I could happily listen to him for hours, whether he's chewing out a malcontent Bill Mauldin: "Oh shut up, you dern little cuss, you little fool. You ain't had that there coat and them pants on for six months, yet you talk as if you was *George* Washington"—or transforming through inflection a handful of monosyllabic dying words into horrifying poetry: "No . . . No . . . Don't touch me . . .

Leave me be . . . Can't you . . . For a minute . . . No . . . No . . . Leave me be . . ." I would be content, indeed, to have heard John Dierkes read from the phone book or, better yet, the index of an American atlas, much as Henry Fonda (speaking of great voices) did on television when—it was shortly after one of the Kennedy assassinations, as I remember—he recited with elegant deliberation a long, long litany of American place names: "Massapequa, Baton Rouge, Crippled Creek, Cincinnati, Salt Lake City, Santa Fe, Metheun, Tallahassee . . . ," proving to everyone fortunate enough to have heard him on that evening that poetry is where you find it.

★

THE BEST
Critic

★

O ur most *important* film critic is Andrew Sarris—he changed the way we look at American movies. James Agee, our *best* film critic, didn't change anything, though he dearly wanted to; the only major film critic who was also a major writer, Agee would have much preferred creating movies to critiquing them. This became increasingly clear in the remarkable series of reviews he wrote for *The Nation* from 1942 to 1948, a body of movie criticism that, in combined eloquence, passion, wit, and insight, has never been equaled. Thanks to a hands-off editor and his own maverick soul, Agee was able to write his column as he saw fit, free of any pressures to cater to the demands of the marketplace or to the aesthetic or political biases of his employers or readership. His reviews were allowed to range in length from a 4,500-word analysis of *Monsieur Verdoux*, serialized over three issues, to a review that was shorter than the title of the movie it was addressing: "*You Were Meant for Me.* That's what you think." He was permitted far enough afield to discuss in detail an Army training film, newsreels of FDR, or a current Warner Brothers cartoon (strange as it seems, when these animated minimasterpieces were first released practically no one with any claim to a brain paid the slightest attention to them)—all in the same unique prose style, pitched somewhere between the conversational and the biblical, he had perfected in *Let Us Now Praise Famous Men*. Agee's writing style, which died with him, was leavened by a kind of flippant wit (Manny Farber called it "aristocratic gashouse humor"), which was commonplace in the 1920s and '30s, was less so in the '40s and '50s, and is now all but extinct. Two examples: "I would like also to recommend *Random Harvest* to . . . any who could with pleasure eat a bowl of Yardley's shaving soap for breakfast"; and, regarding the narrators of Frank Capra's important documentary *Prelude to War*: "Too many of these voices suggest the cheerful drawers peddlers and flunked divinity students who are the normal cantors for our nonfiction films." This latter comment illustrates also Agee's knack for being precise and concise simultaneously, as does this pithy description of Angela Lansbury in *The Picture of Dorian Gray*: "a special kind of short-lipped English beauty . . . evocative of milkmaids in eigh-teenth-century pornographic prints." Agee could make an offhand observation sound almost like immutable law: "Com-edies about snobbism seem, as a rule, to depend on stimulat-ing and playing up to, rather than shriveling, the worst kinds of snobbism in the audience." And I wouldn't mind seeing the following Agee prejudice chiseled in stone or, at least, widely circulated among public-TV programmers: "I believe that political ideas at their most mature and serious are still childish and frivolous as compared with those ideas or concep-tions which attempt to work in, to perceive, and to illuminate, the bottoms of the souls of human beings."

But perhaps Agee's greatest gift was for moral eloquence. When a prominent rabbi, monsignor, and minister teamed up to write a series of articles exhorting the movie industry to discourage its stars from off-lot sexual shenanigans, Agee wrote: "In my opinion such moralists are impudent enough in horning in on what appears on the screen without assuming it is their right and duty, as well, after the stars' working hours, to get into bed with them. I would like to know, moreover, what a few people whose moral sense has reached the shaving age think of arbiters of morals who still believe in the obligation of the prominent to set a good example; who still believe in exerting pressure on them in order that they shall exert pressure on others; and who feel so profound a contempt for the souls and minds of people in general as to dare to approach them through force and through example." You just don't find this kind of cranky, humane high-rhetoric anymore and you're not likely to—unless and until, perhaps,

Wilfrid Sheed should decide to collaborate with Pete Hamill and William F. Buckley, Jr., on a book edited by Bill Moyers.

★

THE BEST
Cameo Appearance by a Director in His Own Movie

★

John Huston's *The Treasure of the Sierra Madre* opens in Mexico, 1925, with Humphrey Bogart, as Fred C. Dobbs, a vagrant American down on his luck, stopping strangers in the street and soliciting them for handouts. Twice he accosts John Huston—a prosperous looking gent in white suit, wide-brimmed hat, and outsized cigar—with these words: "Hey, mister, will you stake a fellow American to a meal?" Twice Huston reaches wordlessly into his pocket and gives Bogart a coin. The third time Bogart makes his pitch, Huston, cigar in mouth, stares at him and says, "Such impudence never came my way. Early this afternoon I gave you money. While I was having my shoes polished I gave you more money. Now you

put the bite on me again. Do me a favor, willya? Go occasionally to somebody else—it's beginning to get tiresome."
Bogart apologizes abjectly and promises never to approach
Huston again. "This is the very last you get from me,"
Huston replies and hands Bogart a coin. "Just to make sure
you don't forget your promise," he says, handing Bogart a
second coin, "here's another peso . . . but from now on you
have to make your way through life without my assistance."
With that, Huston exits the movie, and Bogart—his luck
changed?—goes off in search of bigger bounty.

★

THE BEST
Supporting Performance

★

The Big Knife, a near-delirious attack on Hollywood's high-
salaried slave system of not so long ago, boasts a sup-
porting cast of Rod Steiger, Everett Sloane, Jean Hagen,
Shelley Winters, Wendell Corey, Ilka Chase, Wesley Addy,
Paul Langton (unforgettable), and Nick Dennis. In a crowd
like this, few would single out Wendell Corey for top honors.
But Corey's Smiley Coy grabs my ballot not only for Best in
Show but also for the best supporting performance of all time.
With his low-key, even affable West Coast persona (disguising

a pair of the coldest, deadest eyes you'll ever see), Smiley at first seems like small poison compared to his boss, megalomaniacal studio chieftain Stanley Hoff (Rod Steiger). But Hoff has an insane ego as an excuse for his atrocities. What motivates the deadly cynicism of Smiley Coy is much less clear. Corey brings him to life, if that's the right word, through a less-is-more performance that is intelligent, mysterious, chilling, and thoroughly convincing. His best line: "Life's a queer little man, kiddie."

★

THE BEST
Blonde

★

Her name, in fractured French, means "female blonde". I'm not sure that Blondell was her real name or even that she was a real blonde, but for me the quintessential blonde was, is, and always will be Joan Blondell—not Jean Arthur, the best actress who happened to be a blonde, nor such estimable runners-up as Jean Harlow, Carole Lombard, Ginger Rogers, Veronica Lake, or Teri Garr. Of the four movie-star books I own, only one allots space to Joan Blondell; in the other three she's a victim not of space but taste limitations, having been elbowed out by Barbra Streisand,

Faye Dunaway, and George Raft among other unworthy pretenders.

Probably the only Miss Dallas to have been born in New York City, Blondell and her unique qualities were best displayed in the series of snappy films she made for Warner Brothers (at the rate of better than one per month) in the early '30s. Her specialties were, in her own words, "the happy-go-lucky chorus girl, saucy secretary, flip reporter, dumb-blonde waitress, I'll-stick-to-you broad." I'm inclined to argue with that "dumb"; Blondell's roles may occasionally have been dumb on paper but never on celluloid—her mother wit kept shining through the fog. Nor could she easily portray the victim, the tramp, the babe-in-the-woods, or the hooker with a heart of mush—so strong, honest, true, and sophisticated, in the best sense of the word, was her nature. She was a master of comedy timing (her near-mispronunciation of the name of a certain snotty Miss Rich slays *Footlight Parade* audiences to this day) and when the moment was right she could break your heart without half trying (which was why she could break your heart). In addition to being a superb actress, she was also, in those early days, a knockout. Joan was, I believe the euphemism is, full-figured and her milky-white voluptuousness probably helped to hasten the arrival of the Production Code of 1934; she seemed always in danger of spilling out of something. One unforgettable moment from *Gold Diggers of 1933*—a very brief glimpse of Blondell at a dressing table in lingeried dishabille—is somewhere, I'm sure, activating a VCR freeze-frame button at this very minute. In short and in my opinion, she was the perfect American woman—at least on screen—but nobody seems to have real-

Joan Blondell

ized it then and nobody seems to realize it now. (It seems odd that today, when everyone and his ex-wife is being rediscovered, there is a book devoted to the films of Barbara Lawrence, and deservedly so, but none to those of Joan Blondell.) Off screen she was A-OK too—when the U.S. entered World War II, Joan, at some cost to her career, was one of the few to go forth and entertain the troops *before* the official tours were organized.

Years ago I was a little surprised when my father, whom I had always regarded as a bit of a highbrow, one day confessed to me a major soft spot for Joan Blondell. Many years later I caught her in an early '30s quickie and began to get the message. At one point Joan wrapped her arms around some Warner's contract player and kissed him. For the first and last time while watching a movie, I felt as if *I* were being kissed (I can imagine how the actor felt). Such were the empathetic powers of Joan Blondell.

★

THE BEST
Cartoon Character

★

Akid needs a cartoon character he can call his own. As a lad sadly lacking in Popeye's strength, Bugs's nerve, Mickey's amiability, and Betty's boobs, I found in Daffy's dread something I could immediately relate to. But that was late, not early Daffy Duck. In the beginning everything was just ducky with Daffy, a blissful psychotic mindlessly hoo-hooing his way through life in his natural habitat. Then, somewhere along the way, unaware that half a brain is more dangerous than none at all, he fell from grace and smack into the wide, wide world of neurosis, abandoning pond and marsh for the most far-flung and forbidding vistas of Hollywood, the Wild West, the twenty-first century—anywhere and every-where he didn't belong. Good-bye, Eden; hello, rat race. It was then that Daffy learned exactly what it means to be a drake in a rabbit's world—a world in which the only reward awaiting a duck who is down on his luck is a lifetime supply of thour perthimmonz. And it was then, as Mel Blanc put it, Daffy became "a little egotistical jerk." (It was also then, not coincidentally, that his speech impediment became most pronounced.)

Psychiatrists, I suspect, would be bored to tears by Bugs Bunny—the healthiest and best adjusted of single-cel creatures—despite his vindictive streak ("you realize, of course, this means war") and a trace of genial sadism ("lemme see . . . what can I do to this guy next?"). Daffy, on the other hand, would have them drooling like Pavlov's dog (or was it Fudd's?). Time and time again Daffy is caught up in the classic neurotic continuum of blind ambition, severe miscalculation, sudden panic, total hysteria, bitter defeat, impotent rage ("you're deth*pic*able!"), and, finally, abject despair—time after time, the same old story: Everything ventured, nothing gained. And this, of course, is precisely why we love him: He's just like you and me, only worse.

In the interest of historical accuracy it must be said that Daffy now and then *was* granted a brief moment of glory; in conclusion let us not forget that it was our hero who, in the title role of "The Scarlet Pumpernickel," delivered (to innkeeper Elmer) what might be the most memorable line ever entrusted to a character in an animated motion picture: "My room, bumpkin. I'm pooped."

★

THE BEST
Director

★

Film critic Stuart Byron described a moment of revelation he experienced midway through a Howard Hawks retrospective. He was beginning, as he recalled, to wonder what all the fuss was about—then one day "it all suddenly hit me: at once I understood even the films I had seen—and dismissed—days before. I was hooked on a certain philosophy of cinema and for good." Exactly the same thing happened to me—but in my case enlightenment arrived not by way of Hollywood but from Tokyo.

Yasujiro Ozu directed more than fifty movies in the course of a career that began in the silent days of the late '20s and ended in the high-color era of the early '60s. His finest films were about contemporary families, most of them Tokyo residents, and his pet plot pretext was a semiarranged marriage: A, more or less contentedly single, must decide whether to marry B while virtually the full remainder of the alphabet play matchmaker. As a result of Ozu's narrative single-mindedness ("same sets, same stories, same camera set-ups, same rhythm, same actors even"*), many of his films seem almost interchangeable; to this day, when I buy a ticket for *Late Spring, Early Summer, Early Spring, Late Autumn, Early Au-*

*Tom Milne

Yasujiro Ozu

tumn, or *An Autumn Afternoon*, I'm not sure what movie I'm about to resee.

Ozu spent more than three decades of his life evolving an inimitably ascetic style of filmmaking and by the time he was through he had banished every type of camera movement (pans, dollies, cranes) and traditional transitional devices (wipes, fades, dissolves) from his creative arsenal. And as his style grew sparser his textual universe shrank accordingly—by the time he had reached the peak of his career he was making little else but domestic comedies. Given the American addiction to soap opera and situation comedy, I'm always puzzled when I hear Ozu characterized as "the least Western" of Japanese directors, and Kurosawa as "the most Western." Kurosawa's world doesn't correspond to any West I know of, other than the long gone and substantially apocryphal American Wild West of the nineteenth century. I feel right at home in the kingdom of Ozu, however; I recognize his people and identify with them. I see them every day, following the same insignificant routines: going to work, getting the children off to school, waiting for trains and waiting for more trains, talking too much, talking too much about nothing in particular. Ozu's characters, unlike Kurosawa's, shun precipitous action like the plague. People are always running around like mad in a Kurosawa picture; Ozuites, like the people I know, don't even walk much. Kneeling or sitting down—in parlors, in bars, in offices—is their customary posture. As David Thomson said, "The family relationships he describes are by no means un-Western. Ozu has a sense of pathos that travels easily."

The most powerfully moving moment in all of Ozu occurs in the final half hour of his final film, *An Autumn Afternoon*. An old widower, accompanied by his son, looks in on his daughter moments before her wedding. We are stunned to discover not the cheeky, blue-jeaned teenager of our previous acquaintance but a handsome young woman splendorously adorned in a traditional Japanese bridal costume. *She is crying.* This shattering moment—the moviegoing equivalent of being run over by a tractor in an onion field—can be interpreted virtually any way one wants to. I've heard a feminist suggest that the girl is in despair at the realization that she is about to enter into a state of lifelong marital and domestic bondage—but I prefer to believe that what's going on is a little more complex than that. I read the scene as a bittersweet reflection made by a profoundly conservative man—one who recognized the necessity for change but, like the bride-to-be he created, resented it, resisted it, and was saddened by it.

Every great director, according to Andrew Sarris, fabricates "a self-contained world with its own laws and landscapes." To no director are these words more applicable than Ozu, an artist I cherish (not least for introducing me to one of the cinema's most radiant spirits, the actress Setsuko Hara). If you are unable to connect with Ozu's films, they're likely to strike you as boring, pointless, alienating, and/or reactionary. But if you do respond, these movies may quite possibly change your life. Over the decades, the oeuvres of several filmmakers have proven themselves deserving of the words *exciting, powerful,* or *brilliant*; Yasujiro Ozu is the only director whose body of work can accurately and without qualification be characterized as *therapeutic.*

★

THE BEST
Eccentric Performance

★

O rson Welles movies are famous for their offbeat performances—notably those of Dennis Weaver and Welles himself in *Touch of Evil*, and virtually the entire cast of *Mr. Arkadin*—but Glenn Anders's unsettling portrayal of George Grisby in *The Lady from Shanghai* takes the cake. Frequently photographed in sweaty close-up, Anders plays Grisby as a cross between Grady Sutton and Guinn "Big Boy" Williams, spiked with an occasional touch of Eric-Bloreish fury. A prissy, middle-American yokel with the juicy, fractured voice and repellently intrusive familiarity of a traveling salesman on the verge of a nervous breakdown, Grisby is at his most hilariously horrid singing and sweating his way through a soppy ballad on the deck of a yacht while accompanying himself on the piano. Anders's outrageous performance was reportedly the result of Welles's bullying directorial manner, a ploy to get the most out of his players, and the entire characterization is said to have been based on Nelson Rockefeller, a notion supported by Grisby's fondness for the appellation "fella."

★

THE BEST
Actor

★

Among the many outstanding actors developed by Hollywood, three were giants: James Cagney, Cary Grant, and James Stewart. Of the three Cagney was the most dazzlingly kinetic and Grant was the most immaculately precise; both were innovators who, at their best—Cagney during the Depression years and Grant in the following decade—regularly took audacious acting chances and almost invariably made them pay off. Unlike Cagney (with *The Public Enemy*) and to a lesser extent Grant (with *Sylvia Scarlett*), James Stewart wasn't catapulted into screen immortality by a single performance—he and his career more or less sneaked up on everybody. The talent was discernible from the beginning, but it was a callow talent at first; too often the characters he played seemed smug, righteous, or self-pitying when they should have been confident, determined, or vulnerable. One could sense, however—in the way he met his big emotional scenes head-on—a major actor waiting to be born. At a time when the likes of Spencer Tracy, Fred MacMurray, Ginger Rogers, Henry Fonda, Gary Cooper, even Bing Crosby were perfecting an understated and oblique new technique of film acting—one that ultimately prevailed (at least among Hollywood's male actors)—Stewart's open-wristed mode of emot-

William Edmunds and James Stewart in *It's a Wonderful Life*

ing must have struck some modernists as something of a throwback. Stewart erupted, however, only if and when his scripts allowed for it; generally he went along with the new laid-back style and became so adept at it that his syncopated stammer and gift for seemingly improvised chat became legend. Gradually his familiar, low-key star/character evolved and with it the patented charm, and together they may have slowed his talent down for a while; Destry wasn't his destiny, but it was the kind of thing everyone liked seeing him do and believed he did best.

The war changed him. After five years in the Army Air Corps, he returned to Hollywood and, according to Frank Capra, briefly considered quitting acting, until Lionel Barrymore, on the set of *It's a Wonderful Life*, talked him out of it. Stewart was determined nonetheless to alter his style. "I realized I'd better do *some*thing," he recalled in a 1966 interview with Peter Bogdanovich. "I couldn't just go on hemming and hawing . . . I looked at an old picture of mine—*Born to Dance*—I wanted to *vawmit*! I had to toughen it up." With this decision Stewart launched the second and more important part of his career and was on the way to becoming the world's finest film actor or, at the very least, "the most complete actor-personality in the American cinema" (Andrew Sarris). It soon became apparent that Stewart's greatness was grounded not in his acknowledged skill for playing refined yokels and idealistic patsys but in his mastery of the grand negative emotions: rage, misery, obsession. The familiar charm remained, to be sure, and even at times blossomed (never in the prewar years had Stewart been as seductively likable as he was in *Anatomy of a Murder* and *Harvey*), but a new and darker Stewart was emerging—beginning with his very first postwar movie, in which he staged the screen's most awesomely convincing nervous breakdown ever. Who of us who have seen *It's a Wonderful Life* will ever forget that breakdown or the shocking, heart-stopping line Stewart hurtles at his wife as he's going over the edge: "Why do we have to have all these kids?" Another memorable glimpse of the new Stewart was afforded by the harrowing scene in *The Man from Laramie* in which Stewart, after being restrained by bad-egg Alex Nicol's men, is shot through the hand by Nicol at point-blank range. Now, I have seen (and am all too frequently reminded about) Marlon Brando's "scum-suckin' pig" bit in *One-Eyed Jacks*, but I'd trade that calculated crowd-pleaser any day for the wounded Stewart's next few moments in *The Man from Laramie*. When Stewart fixes his steel-blue eyes on Nicol and says, with as much pain and anger as any actor can be expected to summon, "Why you *scum*," somehow *Jacks* looks juvenile. Ultimately, of course, there is *Vertigo*. Anyone who still doubts the depth and complexity of James Stewart's expressive powers quite simply has not seen this movie. "Despite every hint of the darker side of Stewart," writes David Thomson, "*Vertigo* was still a surprise . . . Stewart's portrayal is frightening in its intensity: a far cry from a man who talked to rabbits." Dark or light, Stewart never lost this intensity or the earnestness that made it possible. Consider the odd, agitated way he informs his friend and patient John Wayne, *The Shootist*, that Wayne is mortally ill. "Yuh have a *cancer. Advanced.*" Stewart seems more appalled by Wayne's encroaching death than Wayne is. I read this disquiet not only as an indication of Stewart's unflagging commitment to high seriousness but also as the generous gesture of a supporting player toward a lead; if a patient's dignosis can so unsettle the physician who delivers it, that patient must be a very valuable individual indeed.

When I was a boy Cary Grant was my fantasy rich uncle and Jimmy Cagney was my fantasy poor uncle, but I recognized in Jimmy Stewart a true son of the middle class—a group I felt lucky and still feel lucky to have been born into. Maybe that's why he's always been my favorite actor.

★

III
ODDS AND ENDS

★

★

THE BEST
Ad Slogan

★

For Fellini's *Satyricon*: "Rome. Before Christ. After Fellini."

★

THE BEST
Production Irony

★

In 1960 United Artists released an adaptation of a genuine heavyweight of American literature, James T. Farrell's *Studs Lonigan* trilogy of novels set on Chicago's Irish-American South Side. Impelled perhaps by budgetary limitations director Irving Lerner chose to work in a semiexpressionistic style that turned out quite well and made *Studs Lonigan* a surprisingly effective film. This is a minority opinion; Farrell didn't like the picture, most of the critics didn't like the

Jack Nicholson, unidentified actress, and Frank Gorshin

picture, and the moviegoing public didn't even bother to show up. One thing everybody agreed about, however, was the inadequacy of the model-handsome boy who was plucked out of Harvard to play the title role. This was no minor flaw; a *Studs Lonigan* without a Studs Lonigan is an exercise in futility. Who should have been cast as Studs? Cagney? Forty years too old. Lee Tracy? Ditto. Only one great actor was the right type and the right age to play the part in 1960. And it really could have, should have happened, because there on the *Studs* set—right under everyone's nose—was a living purloined letter . . . a twenty-two-year-old unknown who had been cast in the role of one of Studs's buddies, Weary Reilly. His name was Jack Nicholson.

★

THE BEST
Reason to Stop Going to Woody Allen Movies

★

They're unbearable. Does anyone, *can* anyone care about the neurotic concerns of a bunch of rootless, insular, egocentric, overeducated, overpaid Manhattanites? These people aren't alienated—they're aliens. Whatever became of *my* Woody?—the one who, when asked by *Playboy* if he harbored any secret sexual perversions, replied, "Yes. I like to chew gum that's already been chewed by a midget."

★

THE BEST

Book

★

There have been more important movie books, but the most successful concurrence of elements (great subject, great text, great design, great illustrations) can be found in *The Fred Astaire & Ginger Rogers Book*. The first thing that strikes you when you open this squarish little volume is the cleanliness and seductive gaiety of Lester Glassner's design—from the bubbly circle motif that encloses many of the pictures, to the vintage sheet-music covers that introduce the book's major chapters, to the two sequences of tiny, page-corner photos that recreate, flip-book fashion, a pair of Fred and Ginger's classic routines. But it's the text by Arlene Croce, a dance critic with a minor in movies, that makes the book invaluable. The first section of her introduction, "A Note on La Belle, La Perfectly Swell Romance," qualifies as the last word on the Astaire-Rogers magic; it is a superb explication of how, during the peak of their partnership, "dancing was transformed into a vehicle of serious emotion between a man and a woman," a phenomenon that "never happened in movies again." The body of the book allots an entire chapter to each of Fred and Ginger's ten films together, each chapter divided into three sections: The Film, The Numbers, Production. Production provides us with a redoubtable display of solid research molded into first-rate historical exposition, and also serves up some of the book's most interesting tidbits: *The Gay Divorcee* started a fad for Venetian blinds; Hermes Pan functioned as a rehearsal partner for both Astaire and Rogers separately ("with Fred I'd be Ginger, and with Ginger I'd be Fred"). In Numbers we find uncannily precise, almost step-by-step descriptions and critiques of every song and/or dance number in the series, these analyses studded with many examples of Croce's admirable way with a phrase ("ratcheting tap clusters that fall like loose change from his pockets") and her great gift for hitting every relevant nail on the head: The reason Ginger Rogers's dancing hasn't dated, writes Croce, is "because it's so refreshingly laconic. It was dancing at its driest and shapeliest; it had nothing of the excesses, nothing of the sweet tooth of its period." Croce, in fact, is one of the finest and most efficient writers of straight prose I know of. It's almost astonishing how much information she can pack into a phrase, a sentence, a paragraph without sacrificing readability—at no point do you feel you're reading an extended *Variety* headline—and when the occasion demands she can summon up more than a touch of the poet. Attention: any publisher in search of a dream project—how about a multivolume critical encyclopedia in which every Hollywood musical number extant is given the Croce treatment . . . by Croce herself, of course?

★

THE BEST

Advice You'll Ever Receive on How to Behave in Old-Movie Theaters

★

Young couples

Arrive late.

Wonder why there's no line.

Hug and kiss frequently during movie.

Sit directly in front of me.

Older couples

Remain totally silent until picture starts.

During opening credits, begin a conversation; continue it until picture ends.

Remain totally silent until next picture starts.

Sit directly behind me.

Single women over fifty

Find that cellophane ball you lovingly constructed as a girl.

Bring it to theater.

Unwrap it during the first film.

Rewrap it during the second film.

Sit directly behind me.

Single guys from the neighborhood

Talk to movie.

Giggle during violent scenes.

Curse during love scenes.

Check crotch periodically to make sure it's still there.

Don't take no crap from *nobody*.

Sit directly behind me.

Senior citizens

Announce first appearance of everyone in cast ("Greta Garbo" . . . "Melvyn Douglas" . . . "Ina Claire" . . . etc.).

Read all on-screen signs, headlines, letters, etc., aloud ("DANGER, ROAD CLOSED" . . . "KANE ELECTED").

Note major plot developments out loud ("He's got a gun" . . . "The sister is at the window").

Sing along with musical numbers.

Uppermiddlebrows

Attend every European comedy you can, particularly the bad ones.

Laugh at unsubtitled dialogue.

Never laugh at subtitled dialogue.

If the director appears in a cameo, laugh loudly to show that you recognize him.

Talk softly so as not to disturb others; fail.

Sit beside me.

Aging counterculturists

Laugh at any American movie made before *Easy Rider*, except the comedies.

Affect bushy hairstyle.

Sit directly in front of me.

On your way out, ask manager to schedule Robert Downey (Sr.) festival.

Cinéastes

Enter theater shrieking *"Focus!"*

Race to your seat as credits begin.

Sit anywhere near me.

Between films look around theater in search of blood brothers.

Find one and discuss plot of next film (which I've never seen) in loud detail.

Carry latest issue of *Variety*.

Collegians (current or lifelong)

Refer to all films as *flicks*.

Attend films of Samuel Fuller, Robert Aldrich, Joseph H. Lewis, and Val Lewton because the titles are silly.

Discover that the films are not as silly as you'd hoped.

Laugh at them anyway.

Keep an eye out for anything remotely resembling a phallic symbol, then laugh knowingly when you spot one.

Bring dinner.

Eat it.

Strange middle-aged men

Get them to let you out for the afternoon.

Dress *very* casually.

Go to matinee.

Change seats frequently.

Talk to movie.

Yawn audibly to express boredom.

Get into long arguments with the similarly afflicted.

The politically correct

Buy two tickets: one for yourself and one for your social consciousness.

Afterward, ask your social consciousness if it approved of the film.

Leave instincts home.

Practice your smug hiss at every opportunity.

All of us

Refuse to patronize revival houses because "I can always see that on TV or rent it."

Wonder why they're all closing.

★

THE BEST
Decade for Foreign Movies

★

In the 1960s, when Hollywood was patting itself on the back for turning out stuff like *Judgment at Nuremberg*, *Ship of Fools*, and *Who's Afraid of Virginia Woolf?*, the rest of the world was on a cinematic spree of unprecedented proportions. This was the decade when France's (mostly) Young Turks came into their own with gems like *Vivre Sa Vie*, *Masculin Feminin*, *Stolen Kisses*, *La Femme Infidèle*, *The Joker*, *Lola*, *Last Year at Marienbad*, *Les Créatures*, *Judex*, *Mouchette*, and *Le Samourai*; Fellini and his fellow Italians gave us *8½*, *Fellini Satyricon*, *Il Posto*, *Mafioso*, *La Visita*, *La Viaccia*, *The Organiser*, *The Tenth Victim*, *The Witches*, and the Dino Risi masterpiece *The Easy Life*; England did its bit with *Saturday Night and Sunday Morning*, *All Night Long*, *The Loneliness of the Long Distance Runner*, *The Servant*, *Sparrows Can't Sing*, *The Knack*, Richard Lester's Beatles movies, *The System* (a.k.a *The Girl-Getters*), *Charlie Bubbles*, and *The Conqueror Worm*; Czechoslovakia produced *Loves of a Blonde* and *Daisies*; Spain allowed Buñuel's *Viridiana* to slip through; Roman Polanski, from opposite ends of Europe, contributed *Knife in the Water*, *Repulsion*, and *Cul-de-Sac*; even Canada got into the act with *The Luck of Ginger Coffey*, *Nobody Waved Good-bye*, and the sublime Geneviève Bujold in *Isabel*; and the legendary Yasujiro Ozu produced his final three masterworks—all this, as the Hollywood flacks used to promise us, and more. Then, in the '70s, a combination of tight money, declining popular taste, and a paucity of up-and-coming directorial talent forced the rest of the world to join America in the pits. Where we've all been languishing ever since.

★

THE BEST
Opening Epigraph (Unused)

★

"One of the most charming characteristics of Homo sapiens, the wise guy on your right, is the consistency with which he has stoned, crucified, burned at the stake, and otherwise rid himself of those who consecrated their lives to his further comfort and well-being so that all his strength and cunning might be preserved for the erection of ever larger monuments, memorial shafts, triumphal arches, pyramids, and obelisks to the eternal glory of generals on horseback, tyrants, usurpers, dictators, politicians, and other heroes who led him, usually from the rear, to dismemberment and death."

—Preston Sturges, *The Great Moment*

★

THE BEST

Movie-Title Acronym

★

I t's a tie, folks!

The	Jesus!
Hollywood	A
Establishment's	Wax
	Shark!
Glorification	
Of	
Downright	
Fascists	
As	
Tragic	
Heroes	
Exceeds	
Reason.	

★

THE BEST
Quiz Book

★

—is Harry D. and Yolanda L. Trigg's *The Compleat Motion Picture Quiz Book*, if only because it offers each of its 260 entertaining quizzes in two versions: one for "buffs" and one for "duffers." My personal favorite, however, is *The Where Book of Movies* by Dale Thomajan—largely because it's the only quiz book with questions I can answer. Thanks to an auction held in honor of the book's publisher by his bank, I now own 400 copies of the damned thing. That's why—if you send the correct answer to the question below (or even the incorrect one) to me at 23 Leroy Street, New York, N.Y. 10014—I most likely will send you a free copy. Just be sure to include a self-addressed 7 × 10 envelope affixed with four first-class stamps.

Q: If you are a high school graduate born in 1955 in a Massachusetts town located just east of Lexington, what classic Western might very well appear on your résumé?

★

THE BEST
Movie Title

★

Saturday Night and Sunday Morning was not an original title; it's also the name of the Alan Sillitoe novel the film was based on. Nevertheless it's an ideal title for a movie, combining the gritty immediacy of a compressed time frame with a certain vague generic grace in a mixture I find irresistible. No matter what they might have called it it still would have been a first-rate picture, but I confess I would see *any* movie called *Saturday Night and Sunday Morning* (sometimes I think *all* movies should be named *Saturday Night and Sunday Morning*). Runner-up: Ozu's *I Was Born, But . . .*

THE BEST
SCI-FI TITLE
It Happened Tomorrow

THE BEST
MUSICAL TITLE
Best Foot Forward

THE BEST
MONSTER-MOVIE TITLE
The Blob

THE BEST
HORROR-MOVIE TITLE
The Curse of the Cat People

THE BEST
CRIME-MOVIE TITLE
The Public Enemy

THE BEST
COMEDY TITLE
Tillie's Punctured Romance

THE BEST
TITLE OF A CAVEPERSON MOVIE
When Women Had Tails

THE BEST
SEQUEL TITLE
For a Few Dollars More

THE BEST
ESTHER WILLIAMS TITLE
Dangerous When Wet

THE BEST
JAYNE MANSFIELD TITLE
Kiss Them for Me

THE BEST
HYBRID TITLE
Carry On Emmanuelle

THE BEST
YIDDISH TITLE?
From Hell It Came

THE BEST
PUN TITLE
Every Little Crook and Nanny

THE BEST
BUGS BUNNY TITLE
"My Bunny Lies Over the Sea"

THE BEST
THREE STOOGES TITLE
"All the World's a Stooge"

THE BEST
FILM NOIR TITLE
Night and the City

THE BEST
HIGH-CONCEPT TITLE
Mars Needs Women

★

THE BEST
Old-Movie Theater

★

Why is Manhattan's Film Forum 2 my repertory cinema of choice? Because it is run by people who know and love movies. Because the quality of its prints and projection is close to exemplary. Because in a good year it will screen over 400 movies that are worth seeing. Because it introduced me to such wonderful films as *Chang*, *Eskimo*, *Virtue*, *Suspira*, *Blood Money*, *Ride Lonesome*, *Sir Arne's Treasure*, and Jacques Demy's *Lola*. Because it opened my eyes to such immortal performers as Clara Bow, Colleen Moore, Marion Davies, and Maxine Sullivan. Because it's one of the few places where you can still see Cinemascope movies in 35mm, silent movies with live musical accompaniment, 3-D movies with glasses, and French movies without Gerard Depardieu. Because for an annual membership fee that pays for itself in a matter of weeks, you can attend a double feature for $4.50. And because it's only a five-minute walk from where I live.

★

BIBLIOGRAPHY

★

Agee, James. *Agee On Film: Reviews and Comments.* Beacon Press, 1964.

Anderson, Joseph L., and Donald Richie. *The Japanese Film.* Grove Press, 1960.

Bogdanovich, Peter. *Pieces of Time.* Arbor House/Esquire, 1973.

Byron, Stuart. "*Auteurism*, Hawks, *Hatari!* and Me," in *Favorite Movies: Critics' Choice*, ed. by Philip Nobile. Macmillan, 1973.

Caldicott, E. E. J. *Marcel Pagnol.* Twayne Publishers, 1977.

Callenbach, Ernest. "*La Jetée*," in *Film Quarterly*, Winter, 1965–66.

Callenbach, Ernest. "Two Dance Films," in *Film Quarterly*, Winter, 1966–67.

Corliss, Richard. *Talking Pictures: Screenwriting in the American Cinema.* Penguin, 1975.

Croce, Arlene. *The Fred Astaire & Ginger Rogers Book.* Outerbridge & Lazard, 1972.

Dickens, Homer. *The Films of James Cagney.* Citadel Press, 1972.

Farber, Manny. *Negative Space.* Praeger, 1972.

Ferguson, Otis. *The Film Criticism of Otis Ferguson*, ed. by Robert Wilson. Temple University Press, 1972.

Fordin, Hugh. *The World of Entertainment: Hollywood's Greatest Musicals.* Avon, 1973.

Godard, Jean-Luc. "No Questions Asked: Conversation with Jean-Luc Godard," in *Focus on Godard*, ed. by Royal S. Brown. Prentice-Hall, 1972.

Goldblatt, Burt. *Newport Jazz Festival.* Dial Press, 1977.

Greene, Graham. *Graham Greene on Film: Collected Film Criticism, 1935–1939.* Simon & Schuster, 1972.

Greenspun, Roger. "*French Cancan,*" in *Favorite Movies: Critics' Choice*, ed. by Philip Nobile. Macmillan, 1973.

Higham, Charles. *The Films of Orson Welles.* University of California Press, 1970.

Higham, Charles, and Joel Greenberg. *Hollywood in the Forties.* A. S. Barnes & Co., 1968.

Kael, Pauline. "Raising Kane," in *The Citizen Kane Book.* Atlantic Monthly/Little Brown, 1971.

Kaminsky, Stuart M. *Don Siegel: Director.* Curtis Books, 1974.

Katz, Ephraim. *The Film Encyclopedia.* Crowell, 1979.

Leaming, Barbara. *Orson Welles: A Biography.* Viking, 1985.

McClelland, Doug. *The Golden Age of "B" Movies.* Bonanza Books, 1981.

McDonald, Gerald D., Michael Conway, and Mark Ricci. *The Films of Charlie Chaplin.* Bonanza Books, 1965.

Medved, Harry, with Randy Dreyfus. *The Fifty Worst Films of All Time (and How They Got That Way).* Popular Library, 1978.

Moskowitz, Gene. "The Wages of Fear," in *Variety*, 29 April 1953.

Milne, Tom. "Flavour of Green Tea Over Rice," in *Sight and Sound*. Autumn 1963.

Mueller, John. *Astaire Dancing: The Musical Films*. Knopf, 1985.

Mugford, Scott. "Bring Me the Head of Alfredo Garcia," in *Movietone News*, 2 July 1975.

Murphy, Kathleen, and Richard T. Jameson. "Bring Me the Head of Alfredo Garcia," in *Film Comment*, Jan–Feb 1981.

Oates, Warren. Interview by Albert Bomar and Alan J. Warren, in *Film Comment*, Jan–Feb 1981.

Powell, Michael. *A Life in Movies: An Autobiography*. Knopf, 1987.

Pryor, Thomas M. *The New York Times*. "Margie", 17 April 1946.

Quinlan, David. *An Illustrated Encyclopedia of Movie Character Actors*. Harmony Books, 1985.

Reisz, Karel, "The Wages of Fear," in *Masterworks of the French Cinema*. Harper & Row, 1975.

Rosenbaum, Jonathan. "Journals: Paris," in *Film Comment*, July–Aug 1974.

Saroyan, William. *The Human Comedy*. Harcourt, Brace and Company, 1943.

Sarris, Andrew, *The American Cinema: Directors and Directions, 1929–1968*. E. P. Dutton, 1969.

Sarris, Andrew. *Confessions of a Cultist: On the Cinema, 1955–1969*. Simon & Schuster, 1971.

Shipman, David. *The Great Movie Stars: The Golden Years*. Hill & Wang, 1970.

Shipman, David. *The Great Movie Stars: The International Years*. Hill & Wang, 1970.

Siegel, Joel E. *Val Lewton: The Reality of Terror*. Viking, 1973.

Steinberg, Cobbett. *Reel Facts: The Movie Book of Records.* Vintage, 1982.

Thomas, Tony, and Jim Terry with Busby Berkeley. *The Busby Berkeley Book.* A & W Visual Library, 1974.

Thomson, David. *A Biographical Dictionary of Film.* Morrow, 1976.

Truffaut, François, with the collaboration of Helen G. Scott. *Hitchcock.* Simon & Schuster, 1967.

Young, Vernon. On Film: *Unpopular Essays on a Popular Art.* Quadrangle/The New York Times Book Co., 1972.